STUDIES IN PASCAL'S ETHICS

ARCHIVES INTERNATIONALES D'HISTOIRE DES IDEES

INTERNATIONAL ARCHIVES OF THE HISTORY OF IDEAS

Series Minor

16

A. W. S. BAIRD

STUDIES IN PASCAL'S ETHICS

STUDIES
IN PASCAL'S ETHICS

by

A. W. S. BAIRD

MARTINUS NIJHOFF / THE HAGUE / 1975

ISBN 90 247 1677 2

PRINTED IN THE NETHERLANDS

CONTENTS

FOREWORD

The aim of these studies is to show how Pascal's moral outlook reflects the influence on his thought of the basic doctrine of the three orders. This does not mean that an attempt is made to classify all Pascal's moral judgements in order to relate them to that doctrine. The intention is rather to distinguish the different moral stances Pascal takes, and to ascertain how far the apparent inconsistencies between them can be explained, if not reconciled, in the light of the orders.

It is made clear at the outset how the three orders form the framework of Pascal's scale of values, with the different orders representing at once categories of moral value and orders of being. The peculiar nature of this scale, in which moral and ontological values coalesce, calls for a double criterion, or variable, to allow for differences both of degree and of kind. Since the criterion of rank in the scale is reality, the assigning of value becomes largely a question of perspective: a quality from a given order taken by itself is real, and has moral value, but when compared with a quality from a higher order it loses both its reality and its worth.

Pascal's fluctuating estimate of natural ethics shows how this relativity inherent in the structure of the orders is reflected also in his judgements of value. Since value depends upon the perspective from which the judgement is made, Pascal is bound to appear to shift his ground: from one point of view acts based on the natural light of reason are accorded positive value, whereas from a different point of view all natural behaviour seems uniformly worthless.

The authoritarian approach to ethics which Pascal adopts in the *Provinciales* follows from the rejection of reason as the guide to conduct, and the denial of moral worth to acts in the natural order. If virtue is confined to the supernatural order, it is clearly necessary to look to some authority with supernatural credentials for moral guidance; and the Christian revelation, guaranteed by tradition, answers this purpose. As a result Pascal denounces Jesuit moral theology, not only because of its reliance on reason, but also because of the Jesuits' willingness to accept the moral ideal of the contemporary nobility as the standard to which they attempt to shape Christian morality. In Pascal's terms this means disregarding the qualitative difference between the natural and supernatural orders, and he is therefore opposed both to the Jesuits, and to the code of aristocratic values with which he believes they are compromising.

Pascal seems to overlook some of the difficulties which result from applying the doctrine of the three orders to moral questions. In keeping with his conviction that virtue belongs to the supernatural order, he sets up the authority of Scripture as the criterion in ethics. But he does not see that to expect an individual to recognize that authority is already to presuppose he is capable, by himself, of making a valid moral judgement, even though the native power to do so is denied him. Pascal also fails to deal adequately with the linguistic problem involved in applying terms like 'justice' to moral qualities proper to both the natural and supernatural orders. Although he argues that such qualities are incommensurable, like the orders to which they belong, he not only uses the same word for both, but quite often takes them himself to mean the same thing.

The teleological approach to ethics, which Pascal favours in the *Pensées,* reinforces the tendency, latent in the doctrine of the three orders, to depreciate natural virtue. The moral worth of an act is determined by its relation to man's end. But since Pascal identifies the end with man's true good, God, who belongs to the supernatural order, good acts are immediately set beyond the scope of man's natural capacity. Virtue is therefore restricted to the range of acts man performs under the influence of divine grace in order to achieve his final satisfaction.

By emphasizing in his moral judgements the aspect of things as seen from the supernatural order, Pascal is able to make the pursuit of the true good appear more imperative, since, compared with it, all other goods seem illusory. The ready acceptance of the Platonic theme in Augustinian theology contributes further to this tendency to deprive the goods which belong to this world of any ethical character. Once again the relativity which characterizes Pascal's estimate of moral value is seen to result from treating value as a perspective of the three orders.

References for the *Pensées* are to the fragment number in the Lafuma (L.) and Brunschvicg (B.) editions. References for all other works by Pascal are to the edition of the *Œuvres complètes* by Jacques Chevalier in the "Bibliothèque de la Pléïade" (C.), and to the "Grands Ecrivains de la France" edition of the *Œuvres complètes* (G.E.).

CHAPTER I

PASCAL'S THREE ORDERS AS THE BASIS
OF A SCALE OF VALUES

It is, I think, true to say that since Chevalier's book, published in 1922,[1] Pascal critics, if they have agreed about nothing else, have generally acknowledged the central place which the doctrine of the three orders, formulated in the *Pensées*,[2] occupies in Pascal's thought. Different views are held as to the origin and development of the idea. The conception seems to me, however, to form a sort of 'leitmotif', running through nearly all Pascal's writings, so that its evolution can be traced from the mathematical source up to the definitive expression in the fragment from the *Pensées*.[3] In order to determine how far Pascal's often seemingly inconsistent estimates of value are to be explained in terms of this basic conception it will be necessary to examine what, if any, relation holds between each of the three orders if we can regard them as orders of value – or, in other words, to see to what extent they can be said to compromise a scale.

It is important, nevertheless, to emphasize that even in the semi-devotional fragment with which we are concerned – one whose object is primarily to bring out the unique quality of Christ the Redeemer – mathematical overtones can be discerned, notably in the use of the terms *ordre* and *grandeur*. And if the full significance of these overtones is to be appreciated, some acquaintance, at least, with the way in which the terms are used in a mathematical context appears to be called for.

The original definition of the term *ordre*, in the sense of category or class, occurs in a subsidiary treatise appended to the *Traité du Triangle Arithmétique,* dating from the end of 1654. Pascal applies the word *ordre* here to a particular type of numerical series arrived at by means of his arithmetical triangle,[4] so that the definition is a formal one de-

---

[1] J. Chevalier, *Pascal,* Paris 1922.
[2] L. 308; B. 793.
[3] Cf. on this a thesis presented to the University of London in 1964.
[4] C. pp. 108-9; G.E. III, p. 466.

noting merely particular arrangements of numbers that enjoy certain properties in common. In this context *ordre* does not imply heterogeneity, since numbers belonging to the second and third orders are formed simply by *addition* of those contained in the first and second orders respectively.

Grandeur likewise first appears in Pascal's vocabulary in a mathematical context. The general rule with which he concludes the short *Potestatum Numericarum Summa* runs as follows:

> ... on n'augmente pas une grandeur continue lorsqu'on lui ajoute, en tel nombre que l'on voudra, des grandeurs d'un ordre inférieur. Ainsi les points n'ajoutent rien aux lignes, les lignes aux surfaces, les surfaces aux solides; ou – pour parler en nombres comme il convient dans un traité arithmétique – les racines ne comptent pas par rapport aux carrés, les carrés par rapport aux cubes ... En sorte qu'on doit négliger, comme nulles, les quantités d'ordre inférieur.[5]

The meaning of the term *grandeur,* as a component of a given order, is clear from this passage. Moreover, the idea of heterogeneity is also emphasized by Pascal's assertion that the magnitudes of lower orders should be disregarded, as if non-existent, when any particular order is in question. And since the relevant portion of the Latin text contains the significant words "inferiores gradus, nullius valoris existentes," [6] it is plain that Pascal not only considers the orders in question to be generically different one from another, but furthermore that he regards their *valor,* their worth in mathematical terms, as wholly dependent upon whether the particular order is considered in itself or in relation to a higher one.

The principle according to which *grandeurs* are classified in different orders is set out in the Euclidean definition of 'homogeneous magnitudes', which Pascal reproduces in the *De l'Esprit Géométrique:*

> Les grandeurs ... sont dites être de même genre, lorsque l'une étant plusieurs fois multipliée peut arriver à surpasser l'autre.[7]

[5] C. p. 1432; G.E. III, p. 367.

[6] C. p. 171; G.E. III, p. 366.

[7] C. p. 589; G.E. IX, p. 265. This definition serves the purpose of clarifying Pascal's previous assertion regarding "... les noms d'unité, binaire, quaternaire, dizaine, centaine, différents par nos fantaisies, quoique ces choses soient en effet de même genre par leur nature invariable, et quoiqu'elles soient toutes proportionnées entre elles et ne diffèrent que du plus ou du moins ..." C. p. 588; G.E. IX, p. 264. There is a striking resemblance in idea between these definitions of heterogeneous orders made up of homogeneous components and the second definition of the first part of Spinoza's *Ethics:* "That thing is said to be finite in its kind ('in suo genere finita') which can be limited by another thing of the same kind. E.g. a body is said to be finite because we can conceive another larger than it. Thus a thought is limited by another thought. But a body cannot be limited by a thought, nor a thought by a body". *Everyman Edition,* London 1910, p. 1.

In order to illustrate what he understands by 'heterogeneous magnitudes' Pascal cites the difference between zero and positive numbers, rest and motion, and continues:

> ... car toutes ces choses sont hétérogènes à leurs grandeurs, parce qu'étant in-finiment multipliées, elles ne peuvent jamais faire que des indivisibles ...[8]

Thus the *grandeurs* included within the scope of any one order are homogeneous, but in relation to those belonging to a different order they are, like the orders which they compose, rigorously heterogeneous. It is clear then that Pascal is making use of analogies drawn from mathematics when he insists, in the fragment from the *Pensées,* on the qualitative distinction separating each of the three orders of being, with the two higher absolutely transcendent in regard to the first, and the third in a similar relation to the second, so that *no* degree or amount of the content of a lower order will ever suffice, of itself, to produce a higher one.

That Pascal envisages the orders as comprising something more than a scheme of reality, will be recognized, I think, if we consider the important criticisms of the conception made by Professor C. C. J. Webb. Webb regards Pascal's insistence on the disparateness of the first two orders of bodies and minds as simply an example of normal Cartesian dualism, and alleges that "the moment one substitutes for bodies as such, bodies regarded as organic to consciousness and thought, you have left the disparateness behind and jumped, so to say, the problems which it raises. Yet this Pascal does when he assigns the life of captains and kings and the glory thereto belonging to the 'order of bodies'." And with respect to the third order of charity, Webb maintains, contrary to Pascal, that "... it is obvious that we are still speaking of *thoughts* and *feelings* ... so that, however superior in value the saint may be to Archimedes and spiritual wisdom to science, the latter is plainly not removed from the former by the same absolute disparateness as lies between a body ... and 'une petite pensée'." [9]

Although these objections are not made without some justification, the fact that Webb appears to have overlooked the partly *moral* connotation of the terms "corps", "esprit", "charité", as Pascal uses them in this context, invalidates much of his criticism. This oversight might have been avoided, and Webb would perhaps have been less inclined to echo Voltaire's verdict on the passage, as a "galimatias" which Pascal would have expunged on revision,[10] if he had considered the fragment along-

---

[8] C. p. 590; G.E. IX, pp. 267-8.
[9] *Pascal's Philosophy of Religion,* Oxford 1929, pp. 108-9.
[10] *Lettres philosophiques,* ed. F. A. Taylor, Oxford 1956, p. 105.

side another one from the *Pensées* which bears upon the same subject:

Concupiscence de la chair, concupiscence des yeux, orgueil, etc. – Il y a trois ordres de choses: la chair, l'esprit, la volonté. Les charnels sont les riches, les rois: ils ont pour objet le corps. Les curieux et les savants: ils ont pour objet l'esprit. Les sages: ils ont pour objet la justice.[11]

This makes it plain, I think, that Pascal conceives of the three orders, not only as orders of being, a point upon which the critics are agreed, but also as moral categories, in which individuals range themselves according to the nature of the end which they pursue as the goal of existence.

And to return to the fragment in question, Pascal nowhere there intimates that when he refers to the qualitative division between the first two orders he has in mind the sort of rigid dualism between matter and thought envisaged by Descartes. Indeed the very fact that he does select persons as exemplifying his orders shows how far this is from being the case. We must allow that Pascal is as well aware as anyone else that it is impossible to refuse all power for conscious thought to the captains and kings who typify the "ordre des corps". What he is concerned to point out here is that they, and those like them, are exclusively preoccupied with material achievement and satisfaction; that they direct all their intellectual, as well as physical, effort to this purely worldly end; and that they are therefore in his own terminology "charnels". Similarly with Archimedes and his fellow-members of the "ordre des esprits"; their lives are wholly taken up with the quest for knowledge to be acquired through the senses and reasoning. And both these types of individuals, characterized by the objects which they set themselves to achieve, are cursed by the purblindness that results from preoccupation.

Moreover, when Webb, in regard to the division between the second and third orders, alleges that in the latter we are still dealing with 'thoughts' and 'feelings', so that the disparity here is not as marked as that between the first and second, he fails to see that in this respect Pascal is primarily concerned with the groundwork and range of the two orders – the groundwork and range of the *natural* set against that of the *supernatural*. The naked human mind is quite capable by itself of carrying out disciplined research into the relations between the phenomena of the visible world, or of wrestling with abstract problems of geometry, *but* no amount of striving on its part will ever suffice to bring it to an awareness of the supernatural. It is the *qualitative* difference between the two that counts here, for all the scientists in the world put

---

[11] L. 933; B. 460.

together would not suffice to produce even the first beginnings of a saint – in Pascal's view it is only by grace, by the inspiration of the Holy Spirit, that this refashioning can be achieved.

As Pascal depicts them, the members of the lower orders just do not see the values prized in the order above their own – their private pursuits act as a kind of film drawn over their eyes, so that their respective fields of vision are limited to the aspect of experience in which they place their end, and seek their fulfilment. And it is plain that, to this extent at least, the terms "corps" and "esprit" are used merely as convenient labels to represent the values characteristic of the particular order.

The way in which the sort of values they pursue in life determines the particular order of being to which various individuals belong, emerges very clearly in connection with the elaborate doctrine of the "figuratifs" worked out in the *Pensées,* and applied especially to the Old Testament prophetic utterances, in order that these may be interpreted as fore-shadowing the advent of Christ. In a letter to Mlle de Roannez,[12] Pascal refers to the failure of the Jews to recognize that certain passages in the Scriptures are figurative in meaning, with the result that they are thereby prevented from seeing the values of the spiritual order upon which such passages are based, and which should be presented to the mind through their agency. Their plight, as it is depicted in the *Pensées,* shows how their attempt to find satisfaction in the values of the 'material' order blinds them to the values of the supernatural order.

Les Juifs ont tant aimé les choses figurantes, et les ont si bien attendues, qu'ils ont méconnu la réalité, quand elle est venue dans le temps et en la manière prédite. Les rabbins prennent pour figures ... tout ce qui n'exprime pas l'unique but qu'ils ont, des biens temporels.
Les Juifs charnels, n'entendaient ni la grandeur ni l'abaissement du Messie prédit dans leurs prophéties. Ils l'ont méconnu dans sa grandeur prédite ... ils ne le croyaient pas si grand qu'il fût éternel. Et ils l'ont méconnu de même dans son abaissement et dans sa mort ... Ils ne le croyaient donc ni mortel, ni éternel: ils ne cherchaient en lui qu'une grandeur charnelle.[13]

The "Juifs charnels", members of the "ordre des corps" as the qualify-ing adjective denotes, unable to see the deeper significance of the "fig-ures", to penetrate to the 'reality' behind them, to set their goal above the 'material' satisfaction afforded by the things of this world, are conse-quently incapable of appreciating the true nature of the spiritual Mes-siah, or the prophecies announcing his coming. In this they illustrate the truth of the claim, made with respect to the supernatural values in the

---

[12] C. p. 510; G.E. VI, p. 89.
[13] L. 270; B. 670. L. 256; B. 662.

three orders fragment, that: "la grandeur de la sagesse . . . est invisible aux charnels et aux gens d'esprit." It is only natural, since they are "charnels", that the "Juifs charnels" should not see beyond the temporal and the material, in fact the mere "figures", for as members of the "ordre des corps" this is their whole world, and not for a single moment can they see beyond it. Their inability to perceive the true spiritual significance of the figures is simply a particular example of that purblindness, characteristic of the preoccupation of members of the two lower orders of being, which renders them incapable of seeing the values prized in the order outside their own.

Moreover, in the scheme of the orders as thus applied, ontological and moral values coalesce, since, by allowing themselves to be ensnared in the figures so that they do not mount beyond them to the reality symbolized, the Jews have become absorbed in what are no more than mere illusions. For Pascal describes and contrasts the two terms "figure" and "réalité" as follows:

Figure porte absence et présence, plaisir et déplaisir.
   Figures. Un portrait porte absence et présence, plaisir et déplaisir. La réalité exclut absence et déplaisir.[14]

Clearly on this view the figure is the bearer of 'presence' and 'pleasure' only when it is treated as a means to lead the mind to something real beyond itself, and is not permitted to draw the attention to itself, thus thwarting the very purpose it is meant to serve. Since in the case of the Jews the figures do not help them to reach the reality behind, but act as snares which prevent the mind from passing beyond, it follows that the values they pursue, seen in what Pascal regards as their true light, can procure only 'absence' and 'displeasure'.

If the values corresponding to the "ordre des corps" and the "ordre de charité" are related in this way as figure or image to reality, it seems reasonable to expect to find a similar relation holding between the orders themselves. Despite the difference in kind between them, upon which Pascal insists, the orders are evidently not too unequal to be compared, since he ranges them in a hierarchy or scale, stating quite plainly that the least amount of the higher order exceeds in value the greatest amount of the lower. A double criterion of degree and kind seems to be called for here, if we are both to do justice to his emphasis on the disparity between the orders, and not convict him of sophistry as a result of disregarding the fundamental principle according to which, as Coleridge puts it, "difference in kind precludes distinction from differ-

---

[14] L. 265; B. 677. L. 260; B. 678.

ence of degree: 'heterogenea non comparari possunt' ".[15] Illuminating in this respect are some remarks which Pascal makes in a letter to Mme Périer, when he contrasts the natural relationship between the members of his family with that established between them by grace.

> ... je trouve que notre bonheur a été si grand d'être unis de la dernière sorte, que nous nous devons unir pour le reconnaître et pour nous en réjouir. Car il faut avouer que c'est proprement depuis ce temps ... que nous devons nous considérer comme véritablement parents, et qu'il a plu à Dieu de nous joindre aussi bien dans son nouveau monde par l'esprit, comme il avait fait dans le terrestre par la chair. ... C'est en quoi nous devons admirer que Dieu nous ait donné et la figure et la réalité de cette alliance; car, comme nous avons dit souvent entre nous, les choses corporelles ne sont qu'une image des spirituelles, et Dieu a représenté les choses invisibles dans les visibles. Cette pensée est si générale et si utile, qu'on ne doit point laisser passer un espace notable de temps sans y songer avec attention.[16]

Especially noteworthy here for the present purpose are the antitheses which derive from the original contrast between nature and grace: "chair – esprit" (in the sense of the spirit of love infused by divine grace), "monde terrestre – nouveau monde" (the Pauline kingdom of the Spirit), "figure – réalité", "choses corporelles – choses spirituelles". The two states envisaged represent respectively the figure and the reality of the bond which unites Pascal and the other members of his family – the natural or biological relation operative in the terrestrial world does no more than symbolize, or point to, the spiritual relation effected by grace in the 'new' world. And this is alleged to be but a particular example of the general principle that corporeal things are only the image of spiritual things, and that God uses visible and natural objects and relationships to symbolize invisible and supernatural ones.

Now, as we have already seen, the chief characteristic of images or figures, as Pascal conceives of them, is that they lack the reality of the objects for which they stand. And it is to this characteristic that he makes oblique reference when he maintains that it is only since they have been conjoined by grace in a spiritual union that the members of his family have been *truly* related to one another. This means in effect that what differentiates the spiritual relationship from the natural, and invests it with greater worth, is the fact that it is real whereas the other is only symbolic, so that in this case *reality* constitutes the value-determinant.

In view of what Pascal says as to the significance and utility of the notion that the natural is an image of the supernatural, and since he

---

[15] *Aids to Reflection*, London 1904, p. 147. cf. C. S. Lewis, *The Discarded Image*, Cambridge 1964, p. 20. The possibility of such a double criterion is discussed by R. G. Collingwood in his chapter on *The Scale of Forms*, in *An Essay on Philosophical Method*, Oxford 1933.
[16] C. pp. 483-4; G.E. II, pp. 248-9.

goes on in the letter to affirm that it is absolutely necessary to envisage the relation between these two classes of things in this way, it seems legitimate to extend reality as the criterion of rank to the orders themselves. In this case the supernatural order of charity, and that which it embraces, is seen as the only mode of being which is fully real, and hence as of immeasurably greater worth than the orders situated, as it were, on the lower confines of reality (for such reality as they have is entirely derivative and reflected); [17] in precisely the same way as the spiritual bond is more valuable and significant in comparison with the natural, by virtue of the fact that it is real whereas the latter is merely figurative and shadows it forth. Yet since Pascal's orders are clearly orders of being, and since it is of the essence of being that it is real, if the criterion of rank in the scale is to be *reality,* this means that the assignment of value becomes largely a question of perspective: a thing from a given order taken by itself is real, and has value, but when compared with something from a higher order it loses both its reality and its worth. Relativism then appears to be inherent in the very structure of the orders, so that it is scarcely surprising that Pascal's judgements of value should exhibit a similar characteristic, if they are indeed based upon that conception.

Further evidence of the importance of reality as a criterion of rank for Pascal's thinking is found in the brief treatise *Sur la Conversion du Pécheur.* The process is there described whereby the soul gradually

---

[17] The point of view which Pascal adopts on this question elsewhere in his writings appears to be that of traditional Christian metaphysics which identifies Being with God. In a letter to Mme Périer he alleges that: "... le péché ... est le véritable néant, parce qu'il est contraire à Dieu, qui est le véritable être ..." C. 485; G.E. II, p. 251. Less important here than the typically Augustinian anhypostatic notion of evil is the resultant conception of being as truly realized only in God, which is again evident in a further letter to Mme Périer at the time of their father's death: "... dans [la mort] par l'anéantissement de la vie, la créature rend à Dieu tout l'hommage dont elle est capable, en s'anéantissant devant les yeux de sa Majesté, et en adorant sa souveraine existence, qui seule existe réellement." C. p. 493; G.E. II, p. 544. The implication which this Christian ontology carries for conceptions of the material universe has been insisted on by M. Gilson: "Si Dieu est l'Etre, il n'est pas seulement l'être total: 'totum esse'; comme on vient de le voir, il est encore l'être véritable: 'verum esse'; ce qui signifie que le reste n'est que l'être partiel et ne mérite même pas véritablement le nom d'être. Voilà donc tout ce qui nous semble au premier abord constituer la réalité par excellence: le monde de l'étendue et du mouvement qui nous entoure, rejeté dans la pénombre de l'apparence et relégué dans la zone inférieure d'une quasi-irréalité". *L'esprit de la philosophie médiévale,* 2nd ed., Paris 1944, p. 63. That such a view does not however rule out completely the possibility of a scale envisaging degrees of reality and value is argued by W. T. Stace in his chapter on *Truth, Reality, Illusion,* in *Time and Eternity: An Essay in the Philosophy of Religion,* Princeton 1952, cf. in particular pp. 125 ff.

becomes aware that the pleasures, relationships and goods of this world, to which it has become attached, are transitory, unreal and valueless when seen from the standpoint of the eternal. As the result of the first influx of divine grace, which it receives, the soul experiences some discomfort:

D'une part, la présence des objets visibles la touche plus que l'espérance des invisibles, et de l'autre la solidité des invisibles la touche plus que la vanité des visibles.[18]

Here again it is the antitheses that are important – the visible objects, although present, are seen to be mere vanity, of no substance or duration; whereas the invisible, although as yet unrealized and still the object of hope, possess the solidity, the reality lacking in the former.

The soul comes to recognize that the perishable things of this world, from which it has so far derived its sole enjoyment, are passing every moment from its grasp, and that in the end it will find itself completely bereft of all on which it has pinned its hopes of happiness.

De sorte qu'elle comprend parfaitement que son cœur ne s'étant attache qu'à des choses fragiles et vaines, son âme se doit trouver seule et abandonnée au sortir de cette vie, puisqu'elle n'a pas eu soin de se joindre à un bien véritable et subsistant par lui-même, qui pût la soutenir et durant et après cette vie.[19]

In this comparison too, between the "bien véritable et subsistant par lui-même", capable of substaining the soul, both during and after this life, on the one hand, and the "choses fragiles et vaines" which cease with this life, on the other, the contrasted pairs of adjectives, "fragiles et vaines – véritable et subsistant", show that it is the reality to which the latter point, as against the necessarily ephemeral nature of whatever the former qualify, that determines the respective value of the two classes of goods. And Pascal alleges further in this context that the claim that things of this world are capable of transmitting any "plaisir solide" is proved to be unfounded by "un nombre infini d'expériences si funestes et si continuelles"; [20] so that once more reality is denied, in the light of the supernatural, to things which properly belong to the "ordre des corps" or the "ordre des esprits", while their relative worthlessness is held to consist in precisely that deficiency.

'Conversion' therefore, in Pascal's terms, requires a definite transition, under the influence of divine grace, from the natural experience of life, embracing the two lower orders, to a new and infinitely higher order, the

[18] C. p. 548; G.E. X, p. 422.
[19] C. p. 549; G.E. X, p. 423.
[20] ibid.

supernatural order of charity. The revaluation of everything which this involves means that, once perceived, the values of this order appear as alone real and, compared with them, everything that previously seemed valuable taken by itself now appears shadowy and illusory. Thus in the seventh letter to Mlle de Roannez Pascal speaks of

... un si grand bonheur et ... un si grand honneur que Dieu leur a fait. Tous les honneurs du monde n'en sont que l'image; celui-là seul est solide et réel ...[21]

The familiar contrast is here made explicit – the superior worth and greater desirability of the supernatural good stems from the fact that it alone is truly real, while the temporal is a mere shadow of it.

However, this 'image-relation', as it may be described, is operative not only between natural and supernatural, in terms of the contrast between the "ordre de charité" and the two lower orders, but also between these two lower orders themselves; between the intellectual and the corporeal. In the fragment from the *Pensées* [22] Pascal implies that it is the cognitive power of the mind which secures for it a superior rank in the scale of being, and in his letter to the Queen of Sweden, in the course of marking the differences between these two lower orders, he affirms:

... et le pouvoir des rois sur les sujets n'est, ce me semble, qu'une image du pouvoir des esprits sur les esprits qui leur sont inférieurs ... Ce second empire me paraît même d'un ordre d'autant plus élevé, que les esprits sont d'un ordre plus élevé que les corps ...[23]

Intellectual dominion, therefore, has the reality lacking in sheer physical dominion, so that in this instance the 'image-relation' emphasizes the superiority of the "ordre des esprits" over the "ordre des corps".

If the three orders *can* be construed in this way, as a scale whose criterion of rank is reality, it still remains to be shown how the conception underlies Pascal's judgements of value. It is obvious, I think, that where a conception is sufficiently basic to act as the background determining a writer's judgement in particular instances, explicit references to it will be rare except when he is concerned to expound it at length. This applies in Pascal's case in regard to the doctrine of different orders of being, but one or two notable examples can be isolated of the way in which it does determine his estimates of value.

The exclusion of justice from the sphere of secular society and politics follows logically from the argument of several fragments in the *Pen-*

---

[21] C. p. 515; G.E. VI, p. 219.
[22] Cf. also L. 200; B. 347.
[23] C. p. 503; G.E. III, pp. 30-1.

sées,[24] and an important parallel occurs in the *Entretien avec M. de Saci.* In his assessment there of the benefits to be derived from a study of the writings of Montaigne and Epictetus, Pascal is reported as saying that:

Montaigne est incomparable pour confondre l'orgueil de ceux qui, hors la foi, se piquent d'une véritable justice ...[25]

The teaching of Epictetus, on the other hand, although it counteracts apathy, has a tendency to induce pride, and on that account may prove harmful to those unaware of:

... la corruption de la plus parfaite justice qui n'est pas de la foi.[26]

And the full significance of this last line in particular for an appreciation of the assumptions underlying Pascal's expressed views on ethics and politics becomes apparent when it is considered alongside a passage taken from a group of fragments usually appended to the *Pensées,* but more closely related in subject matter to the *Provinciales:*

S'ils ne renoncent à la probabilité, leurs bonnes maximes sont aussi peu saintes que les méchantes, car elles sont fondées sur l'autorité humaine. Et ainsi, si elles sont plus justes, elles seront plus raisonnables, mais non pas plus saintes; elles tiennent de la tige sauvage sur quoi elles sont entées.[27]

Now it is clear from these two extracts that with respect to justice, and ethics generally, Pascal is prepared to recognize that on the purely human and secular level varying degrees of such concepts as goodness or justice, and their opposites, are realizable in actions performed, decisions made, etc., that relative to other acts on the same plane certain acts may be adjudged better, more just, more in accordance with what is there regarded as rational behaviour. But, when looked at from the standpoint of acts characteristic of the supernatural order, these relative differences are so slight as to be negligible; so that from *this* point of view two adjacent acts on the natural level, one of which is good, the other bad relatively to each other, will appear indistinguishable. The goodness in question will not merely be an inferior sort of goodness, but will not be goodness at all in the sense which that word connotes in the supernatural order.

As Pascal was probably aware, he might have appealed to St Augustine in justification of this habit of thinking on two levels, as Chesterton aptly put it once,[28] and of assigning value accordingly. For Au-

[24] Cf. L. 60; B. 294. L. 520; B. 375. L. 85; B. 878.
[25] C. p. 574; G.E. IV, pp. 55-6.
[26] *ibid.*
[27] L. 916; B. 920.
[28] G. K. Chesteron, *Chaucer,* 2nd ed., London 1948, p. 270.

gustine, even if he does not go so far as to say that, viewed from the supernatural order, secular virtues and vices appear on a par, none the less contrasts the two planes on occasion in such a way as to imply that what is characteristic of the lower taken by itself has value, but that it loses this value when it is compared to the higher.[29]

But in any case such an approach on Pascal's part testifies not merely to the influence on his thinking of the basic notion of the orders, but also to the very mathematical mould in which his mind is cast, and to the extent to which his terms of reference, regardless of the particular context, are instinctively mathematical. For these extracts provide an example of the application of the general principle enunciated at the end of the short treatise entitled *Potestatum Numericarum Summa* – that a continuous magnitude of a given order is not increased by the addition to it of any number of magnitudes of a lower order; points add nothing to lines, lines add nothing to surfaces, etc.:

En sorte qu'on doit négliger, comme nulles, les quantités d'ordre inférieur.

However, Pascal offers no justification, and doubtless it never crossed his mind that any was necessary, for this transference of the relation holding between mathematical concepts to the field of morals.

[29] Cf. for example the following passage from *The City of God,* V, 19: "... no man can have true virtue without true piety, ... nor is that virtue true either, when it serves but for human ostentation. But those that are not of the eternal city ... the city of God, are more useful to their earthly city in possessing that purely world-respecting virtue, than if they lacked that also. ... But let that virtue that serves human glory without piety be never so much extolled, it is not comparable even with the imperfect beginnings of the saints' virtues, whose assured hope stands fixed in the grace and mercy of the true God." *Everyman Edition,* London 1945, vol. 1. pp. 169-70. Etienne Gilson notes that "Saint Augustin marque toujours soigneusement: 1 Que les vertus des païens, bien qu'elles soient des vertus morales réelles, ... 2 Ces vertus naturelles sont stériles de toute valeur surnaturelle." *Introduction à l'étude de Saint Augustin,* 2nd ed., Paris 1943, p. 198, n.l.

CHAPTER II

PASCAL'S AMBIVALENT ATTITUDE
TOWARD NATURAL MORALITY

I. THE *PENSÉES* AND MINOR WORKS

Madame Périer, in her account of Pascal's life, records that before reaching his twenty-fourth year her brother had abandoned his scientific researches in order to devote himself entirely to religious pursuits.[1] Chronologically this claim has no foundation. But there is evidence in Pascal's own writings of a shift of emphasis, from the study of the sciences to that of questions relating to man's condition and destiny, which undoubtedly represents a watershed in his intellectual development. This evidence, in the form of express statements of a change of interest and of judgements as to the relative worth of these two pursuits, shows conclusively that Pascal came to regard morals as more important than mathematics and natural science.[2]

The transition seems to result in part from Pascal's growing conviction of the irrelevance of mathematics and physics. His own writings on these subjects are notable for their lack of reference to practical application. The highly abstract nature of his mathematics perhaps explains the deficiency there.[3] But even in physics the emphasis on utility of

---

[1] *La vie de Monsieur Pascal,* C. p. 7; G.E. I, pp. 58-9. For a balanced discussion of the historical accuracy of this claim cf. J. Mesnard, *Œuvres complètes de Blaise Pascal,* vol. I, Paris 1964, pp. 566-9.

[2] Cf. *De l'esprit géométrique,* C. p. 591; G.E. IX, pp. 269-70. Letter to Fermat, August 1660, C. p. 522; G.E. X, p. 4. *Pensées,* L. 136; B. 139. L. 687; B. 144. L. 23; B. 67. L. 84; B. 79. L. 164; B. 218. L. 150; B. 226.

[3] The only specific reference to the utility of mathematics which I have found occurs at the end of the brief *Numericarum potestatum generalis resolutio,* usually appended to the treatise on the arithmetical triangle. Pascal writes there: "Horum demonstrationem, paratam quidem, sed prolixam etsi facilem, ac magis taediosam quam utilem supprimimus, an illa quae plus afferunt fructus quam laboris vergentes." C. p. 147; G.E. III, pp. 554-5.

discoveries is surprisingly slight given the climate of the age.[4] Unlike Bacon and Descartes,[5] Pascal does not set out to study nature primarily in order to extend man's control over it. His writings betray none of the hope that animates theirs that the growth of scientific knowledge will result in the relief of man's estate by harnessing nature to his purposes. Nor is this the end which he looks to in striving after a fuller and surer

[4] In the *Récit de la grande expérience* he alleges that in the projected *Traité du vide* he will deduce "conséquences ... aussi utiles que curieuses" from the results of the experiment performed on the Puy de Dôme. C. p. 400; G.E. II, pp. 368-9. Again in the first letter to M. de Ribeyre he claims of this experiment that: "Les conséquences en sont très belles et très utiles." C. p. 409; G.E. II, p. 494. In an additional *Fragment* Pascal propounds a rule for certain of the variations which occur in the effects produced by atmospheric pressure as a result of varying weather conditions, and notes "Cette connaissance peut être très utile aux laboureurs, voyageurs, etc., pour connaître l'état présent du temps, et le temps qui doit suivre immédiatement, mais non pas pour connaître celui qu'il fera dans trois semaines: mais je laisse les utilités qu'on peut tirer de ces nouveautés, pour continuer notre projet." C. p. 467; G.E. II, p. 523. Although the fragment concludes here, so that it is not possible to determine the precise nature of the "project" to which Pascal alludes, it is highly significant that he should deliberately neglect in this way to pursue a line of enquiry which promises to be fruitful in practical advantages. Finally, the opening lines of the dedicatory letter for the arithmetical machine show that considerations of utility played some part in its conception: "Si le public reçoit quelque utilité de l'invention que j'ai trouvée pour faire toutes sortes de règles d'arithmétique par une manière aussi nouvelle que commode, ..." C. p. 349; G.E. I, p. 298.

[5] In the final aphorism of the *Novum Organon* (II, 52) Bacon maintains that, consequent on the "emancipation" and "coming of age" of the human understanding effected by his new method of discovery, "there cannot but follow an improvement in man's estate and an enlargement of his power over nature." The Fall resulted in man being deprived of his dominion over creation, but this can be in some part repaired "by arts and sciences. For creation ... is now by various labours ... at length and in some measure subdued to the supplying of man with bread; that is, to the uses of human life." *The Philosophical Works of Francis Bacon*, ed. J. M. Robertson, London 1905, p. 387. Descartes's dominant concern to promote the welfare of mankind through the study of the sciences is attested notably in the sixth part of the *Discours de la méthode*. He there alleges that on recognizing the scope and novelty of some "notions générales touchant la physique," reached through the application of his method, "j'ai cru que je ne pouvais les tenir cachées sans pécher grandement contre la loi qui nous oblige à procurer autant qu'il est en nous le bien général de tous les hommes. Car elles m'ont fait voir qu'il est possible de parvenir à des connaissances qui soient fort utiles à la vie, et qu'au lieu de cette philosophie spéculative qu'on enseigne dans les écoles, on en peut trouver une pratique, par laquelle, connaissant la force et les actions du feu, de l'eau, de l'air, des astres, des cieux et de tous les autres corps qui nous environnent, ... nous les pourrions employer en même façon à tous les usages auxquels ils sont propres, et ainsi nous rendre comme maîtres et possesseurs de la nature." This is desirable not only in order that man may be able to take advantage of the opportunities which the physical world offers, "... mais principalement aussi pour la conservation de la santé, laquelle est sans doute le premier bien et le fondement de tous les autres biens de cette vie; ..." This explains Descartes's intention to devote "his whole life" to the study of medicine – "une science si nécessaire." Descartes, *Œuvres et lettres*, ed. A. Bridoux, Paris 1953, pp. 168-9.

way of interpreting nature. In the *Préface pour le traité du vide* Pascal refers to human reason as a stored consciousness capable of indefinite development and increase of content, and insists on the analogous continual overall increase and advance of the body of mankind's scientific knowledge.[6] But even here there is nothing to indicate that he believes any improvement of man's lot will follow on such progress.

In view of the limited scope of Pascal's own scientific interests, and since he seems never to have entertained the prospect of a scientific morals such as Descartes looked forward to achieving,[7] it is not altogether surprising to find him claiming in the *Pensées*

J'avais passé longtemps dans l'étude des sciences abstraites; et le peu de communication qu'on en peut avoir m'en avait dégoûté. Quand j'ai commencé l'étude de l'homme, j'ai vu que ces sciences abstraites ne sont pas propres à l'homme, ... et que [l'étude de l'homme] est la vraie étude qui lui est propre.[8]

The conclusion to the first section of the treatise *De l'esprit géométrique*, where Pascal displays profound admiration for both the subject-matter and method of geometry, already foreshadows this attitude. One of the advantages held out to those capable of perceiving that motion, space and number have infinite potential for addition and division is that this will enable them to appreciate nature's power and greatness in the two-fold infinity observable on all sides, and so help them to come to know themselves. By making man aware of his own physical position in the natural scheme geometry will prompt him to moral reflection which is worth more than "tout le reste de la géométrie même." [9]

By August 1660 Pascal is not prepared to allow even this subservient function to geometry. In a letter to the mathematician Fermat he writes

Car pour vous parler franchement de la géométrie, je la trouve le plus haut exercice de l'esprit; mais en même temps je la connais pour si inutile, que je fais peu de différence entre un homme qui n'est que géomètre et un habile artisan.[10]

Despite the continuing influence exercised by mathematics on Pascal's own approach to moral questions, as one of the basic factors shaping his canons of thought, he judges it useless for that purpose here.

The place which the notion of "honnêteté" occupies in his thought reflects in some degree this change of outlook on Pascal's part. In the

---

[6] C. pp. 533-5; G.E. II, pp. 137-143.
[7] Cf. the *Lettre de l'auteur à celui qui a traduit le livre*, intended as a preface for *Les principes de la philosophie, Œuvres et lettres*, ed. Bridoux, pp. 565-570, and P. Mesnard, *Essai sur la morale de Descartes*, Paris 1936, pp. 24-34.
[8] L. 687; B. 144.
[9] C. p. 591; G.E. IX, p. 270.
[10] C. p. 522; G.E. X, p. 4.

letter to Fermat, for example, Pascal acknowledges Fermat's pre-eminence in mathematics, but goes on to depreciate it as a quality proper to a mere "métier".[11] It is Fermat's "honnêteté" that now attracts Pascal to him, for it is a quality which merits esteem.[12] There is an interesting contrast between Pascal's attitude in this letter and his previous correspondence with Fermat. The earlier letters are entirely taken up with mathematical questions, and on one occasion Pascal actually remarks, when describing a person whose "honnêteté" he himself admits is unrivalled, that this man's ignorance of geometry is "un grand défaut".[13] By contrast with the specialist tendency of the geometer, whose "métier" absorbs his whole attention, it is the universal character of the "honnête homme" which now wins Pascal's approval. The "honnête homme" alone proves able to adapt himself to, and so satisfy, the manifold needs of his fellows.

L'homme est plein de besoins: il n'aime que ceux qui peuvent les remplir tous. 'C'est un bon mathématicien', dira-t-on. – Mais je n'ai que faire de mathématiques: il me prendrait pour une proposition. – ... Il faut donc un honnête homme qui puisse s'accommoder à tous mes besoins généralement.[14]

Pascal's preference for the "honnête homme" is not however determined solely by this quality of "universalité". The "honnête homme" establishes his superiority in the sphere of aesthetics by the "finesse" which enables him to perceive the "modèle naturel" and adopt it as his criterion.[15] But "finesse" relates to morals as well as to aesthetics, and Pascal clearly sees the "honnête homme" as the exponent of the "modèle naturel" in conduct as well as in literary style. The connexion is made plain in a fragment from the *Pensées*.

Géométrie, finesse. – La vraie éloquence se moque de l'éloquence, la vraie morale se moque de la morale; c'est-à-dire que la morale du jugement se moque de la morale de l'esprit, qui est sans règles.
Car le jugement est celui à qui appartient le sentiment, comme les sciences appartiennent à l'esprit. La finesse est la part du jugement, la géométrie est celle de l'esprit.[16]

There seems to be no justification for Brunschvicg's opinion that the relative clause in the first paragraph, "qui est sans règles", applies to

[11] C. p. 522; G.E. X, p. 5.
[12] *Trois discours sur la condition des grands,* C. p. 619; G.E. IX, p. 370.
[13] C. p. 80; G.E. III, p. 388.
[14] L. 605; B. 36. Cf. L. 195; B. 37. L. 587; B. 34. L. 647; B. 35.
[15] Cf. my article on *The 'honnête homme' and aesthetics in the Pensées, Aumla,* 28, 1967, pp. 203-214.
[16] L. 513; B. 4.

the "morale du jugement" and not to the "morale de l'esprit".[17] Quite apart from grammatical and stylistic arguments against such a clumsy usage, the fragment makes much better sense in Pascal's terms if true ethics, based on "jugement", is regarded as superior because any rational ethics must lack "règles." [18] The gist of the passage is clear enough; according to Pascal there can be no true ethics which depends on "esprit", a term used here exclusively of the faculty responsible for discursive reasoning. Since ethics belongs to the domain of "sentiment" and "jugement" the discursive reason will be unable to discover there any 'palpable' principles from which to draw its inferences. In this field judgements must be made spontaneously, "d'une vue", without resorting to the apparatus of definition and logical demonstration.[19]

Pascal is not concerned here to debate the possibility of a morality conceived in purely natural terms. The fragment simply takes that for granted. True ethics belongs, like true eloquence, to the sphere of "finesse" and "jugement". Knowledge of it must therefore be accessible to man's, or at least to the "honnête homme's", natural faculties without the aid of divine grace, and no supernatural sanctions will be required to ensure that its precepts are carried out. The same point is made in another fragment from the *Pensées*.

Ceux qui sont dans le dérèglement disent à ceux qui sont dans l'ordre que ce sont eux qui s'éloignent de la nature, et ils la croient suivre: comme ceux qui sont dans un vaisseau croient que ceux qui sont au bord fuient. Le langage est pareil de tous côtés. Il faut avoir un point fixe pour en juger. Le port juge ceux qui sont dans un vaisseau; mais où prendrons-nous un port dans la morale? [20]

According to this passage nature is the yardstick by which conduct must be judged, although difficulties arise over the question as to what, in a given instance, the natural act will be. The important point however is that Pascal implies that conformity to nature produces ordered behaviour and therefore right action. Despite appearances then he is not echoing the sceptic's stock objection here that what may be natural for one person will not necessarily be so for another, so that an ethics based on

[17] Blaise Pascal, *Pensées et opuscules*, ed. L. Brunschvicg, 7th ed., Paris 1914, p. 321, n.l. Cf. also J. Laporte, *Le cœur et la raison selon Pascal*, Paris 1950, p. 67, n.l.

[18] One of the previously unedited "pensées" published by M. Jean Mesnard in 1962 seems to bear out this interpretation: "Les philosophes de l'Ecole parlent de la vertu et les rhéteurs de l'éloquence sans les connaître. Présentez aux uns un homme véritablement vertueux mais sans éclat, et aux autres un discours plein de beautés naturelles mais sans pointes: ils n'y entendront rien." *Blaise Pascal : Textes inédits*, Paris 1962, pp. 32-3.

[19] L. 751; B. 3. Cf. L. 512; B. 1.

[20] L. 697; B. 383.

nature as the source of order and standard of action will not be susceptible of any positive test. The external criterion, the "point fixe", nature,
is accessible to those who, like the "honnête homme", have the "finesse"
needed to discern it. As Pascal insists in the *De l'art de persuader*

Rien n'est plus commun que les bonnes choses: il n'est question que de les
discerner; et il est certain qu'elles sont toutes naturelles et à notre portée, et même
connues de tout le monde. Mais on ne sait pas les distinguer. Ceci est universel.
Ce n'est pas dans les choses extraordinaires et bizarres que se trouve l'excellence
de quelque genre que ce soit. On s'élève pour y arriver, et on s'en éloigne: il faut
le plus souvent s'abaisser. ... La nature qui seule est bonne, est toute familière et
commune.[21]

Some idea of the kind of questions that such a natural ethics is concerned with is given in the *Pensées*.

Vanité des sciences. – La science des choses extérieures ne me consolera pas de
l'ignorance de la morale, au temps d'affliction; mais la science des mœurs me
consolera toujours de l'ignorance des sciences extérieures.[22]

The expression "la science des mœurs", used here as a synonym for
"la morale", may well have been chosen in part with an eye to the
symmetry of the sentence. But the fact that Pascal does use it in the
second clause, in place of the noun "morale", makes it clear that he conceives of ethics as dealing with practical questions relating to conduct
and life, rather than with the search for a rational basis for such conduct,
or with abstract notions of duty or justice. This preoccupation with the
practical aspect of morals comes out very plainly in another short fragment.

Il faut se connaître soi-même: quand cela ne servirait pas à trouver le vrai, cela
au moins sert à régler sa vie, et il n'y a rien de plus juste.[23]

As it stands this extract implies that the business of ordering one's life,
in Pascal's view the primary concern of ethics, presupposes no external
aid of any kind, even in the shape of a set of rules prescribing right
conduct. That such practical measures are possible for man in his native
capacity, and that they should be grounded in the sort of experience
common to all men, is the force of the passage already considered from
the conclusion to *De l'esprit géométrique*.[24] And the notion that nature,
if attended to, represents an adequate guide on moral questions appears
to lie behind the following fragment from the *Pensées:*

[21] C. p. 602; G.E. IX, p. 288.
[22] L. 23; B. 67.
[23] L. 72; B. 66.
[24] C. p. 591; G.E. IX, p. 270.

L'Ecriture a pourvu de passages pour consoler toutes les conditions, et pour intimider toutes les conditions.

La nature semble avoir fait la même chose par ses deux infinis, naturels et moraux; car nous aurons toujours du dessus et du dessous, de plus habiles et de moins habiles, de plus élevés et de plus misérables, pour abaisser notre orgueil, et relever notre abjection.[25]

Nature therefore, by means of the infinite diversity of types and corresponding range of abilities that characterize the individuals who make up the human race, sets forth what amounts to an admirable system of checks and counter-balances. Attention to these will restore man to a state of equilibrium when he indulges in excesses, and make plain the sort of conduct which befits his condition.

Pascal seems to be in no doubt about the moral quality of the acts which result from following nature's guidance. Even when, despite his claim that "naturellement on aime la vertu, et on hait la folie," [26] he asserts that for man to continue in a virtuous state he must use the method of counterpoise,[27] there is no suggestion that the virtue in question is not a purely natural quality.

Nous ne nous soutenons pas dans la vertu par notre propre force, mais par le contrepoids de deux vices opposés, comme nous demeurons debout entre deux vents contraires: ôtez un de ces vices, nous tombons dans l'autre.[28]

In fact since the method of counterpoise is necessary only in order to keep in the right path so to speak, it follows that virtue is attained by man's own native capacity in the first place. This conclusion coincides with the definition of virtue in the *Trois discours sur la condition des grands,* where it is cited as an example of the "grandeurs naturelles", and is therefore to be regarded as a genuine and effective quality of the soul.[29]

Despite his readiness to admit that the "honnête homme" at least can attain to virtue through the exercise of his own native powers, such apparent optimism about human nature does not prevent Pascal from denying value to natural virtue in other contexts. In the *Entretien avec M. de Saci,*[30] for example, and again in the *Pensées,*[31] he condemns Montaigne's whole approach to morals as pagan. Yet the passage from

---

[25] L. 800; B. 532.
[26] L. 634; B. 97.
[27] The expression is used by Professor A. O. Lovejoy in his *Reflections on Human Nature,* Baltimore 1961, ch. II, where he shows that the device is a common one in the writings of 17th and early 18th century moralists.
[28] L. 674; B. 359.
[29] C. p. 618; G.E. IX, p. 969.
[30] C. p. 569; G.E. IV, p. 49.
[31] L. 680; B. 63.

the essay *De l'institution des enfans,* on which Pascal draws for the description of Montaigne's notion of virtue,[32] is also the one which inspires the conclusion to his own *De l'esprit géométrique.* There he echoes Montaigne's declaration of faith in nature as a guide, and joins him in denouncing what Montaigne regards as the scholastic approach which always represents the good as inaccessible.[33]

The indictment in the *Entretien* of Epictetus's version of the Stoic philosophy, as "principes d'une superbe diabolique", involves Pascal in a wholesale rejection of the possibility of a natural ethics. The offending principles are outlined as follows:

Il dit que Dieu a donné à l'homme les moyens de s'acquitter de toutes ses obligations; que ces moyens sont en notre puissance; ... que l'esprit ne peut être forcé de croire ce qu'il sait être faux, ni la volonté d'aimer ce qu'elle sait qui la rend malheureuse; que ces deux puissances sont donc libres, et que c'est par elles que nous pouvons nous rendre parfaits; que l'homme peut par ces connaissances parfaitement connaître Dieu, l'aimer, lui obéir, lui plaire, se guérir de tous ses vices, acquérir toutes les vertus, se rendre saint ainsi et compagnon de Dieu.[34]

There is nothing particularly remarkable in the explanation Pascal gives to account for these errors, as they appear to him. Epictetus simply failed to realize that man is essentially a fallen creature, and, unaware of man's corruption, on discerning traces of his former "grandeur" he treated human nature as intrinsically sound.[35] Pascal's refusal to endorse Epictetus's tenets stems from his conviction that the Fall has had such far-reaching effects on human nature as to make it inconceivable that man should attain to any good through his own efforts. This clearly rules out the sort of natural code proposed by Epictetus.[36]

Pascal again comments on Epictetus's ethical teaching in the *Pensées.*

Quand Epictète aurait vu parfaitement bien le chemin, il dit aux hommes: 'Vous en suivez un faux'; il montre que c'en est un autre, mais il n'y mène pas. C'est celui de vouloir ce que Dieu veut; Jésus-Christ seul y mène: 'Via veritas'. Les vices de Zénon même.[37]

---

[32] *Les Essais de Michel de Montaigne,* ed. P. Villey, Paris 1965, pp. 160-1.

[33] C. p. 602; G.E. IX, pp. 288-90.

[34] C. p. 563; G.E. IV, p. 36.

[35] C. p. 571; G.E. IV, p. 52.

[36] The most Pascal will concede in the way of benefits to be derived from a combined study of Epictetus and Montaigne is summed up in the judgement that this cannot lead to virtue "mais seulement troubler dans les vices: ..." C. p. 574; G.E. IV, p. 56. On the apologetic purpose of the *Entretien* cf. H. Gouhier, *Blaise Pascal commentaires,* Paris 1966, pp. 90-98.

[37] L. 140; B. 466. Pascal had already emphasized in the *Entretien* that "[Epictète] ne se lasse point de répéter que toute l'étude et le désir de l'homme doit être de reconnaître la volonté de Dieu et de la suivre." C. p. 563; G.E. IV, p. 34.

The conjectural preterite used in the first clause here seems to allow that Epictetus is justified in one of his claims mentioned in the *Entretien,* that man's mind is quite 'free', and able to direct him on moral questions. Such an admission on Pascal's part is not perhaps as startling in this context as may at first sight appear, for he has already acknowledged in the *Entretien* that Epictetus "a si bien connu les devoirs de l'homme".[38] Moreover, the proof of original sin in the *Pensées,* drawn from the paradoxes discernible in human nature, depends for its cogency on recognition of the fact that man combines a real awareness of what constitutes his true nature and end with an impotence to realize them. Several passages testify directly to the hiatus between the knowledge of the good accessible to man and the power to do it which he lacks.

Toutes les bonnes maximes sont dans le monde; on ne manque qu'à les appliquer.[39]

... il y a bien des gens qui voient le vrai, et qui n'y peuvent atteindre.[40]

It is in his other claim – that man's will is equally free, and that his natural powers suffice to ensure him access to and perseverence in the state of highest virtue – that Epictetus shows his ignorance of the actual condition of human nature. Even if the will is hindered in carrying out the directions of the mind by the natural appetites, Epictetus believes that it cannot be actively misled by them. But Pascal's objection is that the will is already perverted, and refuses to go against natural impulses when these prompt man in the wrong direction. Epictetus, therefore, may act as a signpost to the right path, since he is aware of the true end of human nature, but neither he nor any other philosopher can lead man along it. In Pascal's opinion a supernatural aid is needed for that purpose, because mere self-discipline, such as Epictetus recommends, is insufficient to overcome the corrupt will.

A short fragment from the *Pensées* completely undermines any doctrine that holds up obedience to, or conformity with, nature as an ethical maxim.

Quand la malignité a la raison de son côté, elle devient fière. ... Quand l'austérité ou le choix sévère n'a pas réussi au vrai bien, et qu'il faut revenir à suivre la nature, elle devient fière par ce retour.[41]

---

[38] C. p. 563; G.E. IV, p. 35.
[39] L. 540; B. 380.
[40] L. 692; B. 915. Cf. from the same group of fragments dealing with casuistry: "Encore qu'on ne puisse assigner le juste, on voit bien ce qui ne l'est pas." L. 729; B. 931.
[41] L. 537; B. 407.

This passage implies both that evil is natural to man, and that the moral worth of any act derives from the stern effort it involves to overcome the impulse to follow nature. Pascal believes that human nature has become corrupt since the Fall, so that what good actions man may perform will be carried out in opposition to his natural inclinations.

Nor are passages lacking where he expressly states that vice in some form or other is natural to man in his present condition.

... le vice, qui nous est naturel, ...[42]

L'homme n'est donc que déguisement, que mensonge et hypocrisie, ... et toutes ces dispositions, si éloignées de la justice et de la raison, ont une racine naturelle dans son coeur.[43]

Du désir d'être estimé de ceux avec qui on est. – L'orgueil nous tient d'une possession si naturelle au milieu de nos misères, ...[44]

... les vertus nous sont étrangères, ...[45]

Si l'on ne se connaît plein de superbe, d'ambition, de concupiscence, de faiblesse, de misère et d'injustice, on est bien aveugle.[46]

Since virtue consists in thwarting natural impulses it is not surprising that Pascal maintains external aid is necessary for man to attain to it in this state. In contradiction to what he says in the *Entretien* in praise of Epictetus's moral insight, in the *Pensées* he notes that

La vraie nature de l'homme, son vrai bien, et la vraie vertu, et la vraie religion, sont choses dont la connaissance est inséparable.[47]

Elsewhere he goes even further and alleges that:

Sans Jésus-Christ, il faut que l'homme soit dans le vice et dans la misère; avec Jésus-Christ, l'homme est exempt de vice et de misère. En lui est toute notre vertu et toute notre félicité; hors de lui n'y a que vice, misère, erreurs, ...[48]

---

[42] L. 924; B. 498.
[43] L. 978; B. 100.
[44] L. 628; B. 153.
[45] L. 948; B. 668.
[46] L. 595; B. 450.
[47] L. 393; B. 442.
[48] L. 416; B. 546. Cf. also L. 417; B. 548: "Hors de Jésus-Christ nous ne savons ce que c'est ni que notre vie, ... ni que Dieu, ni que nous-mêmes." L. 189; B. 547: "Hors de [Jésus-Christ] et sans l'Ecriture, sans le péché originel, ... on ne peut ... enseigner ni bonne doctrine ni bonne morale." L. 45; B. 83: "L'homme n'est qu'un sujet plein d'erreur, naturelle et ineffaçable sans la grâce." L. 600; B. 440: "La corruption de la raison paraît par tant de différentes et extravagantes mœurs. Il a fallu que la vérité soit venue, afin que l'homme ne véquit plus en soi-même." Pascal is obviously alluding here to the passage in St. John's Gospel where it is alleged that "grace and truth came by Jesus Christ." (1.17) Again in the 7th letter to Mlle de Roannez he maintains that "vertu" is a product of "piété" C. p. 516; G.E. VI, p. 222, and in the *Pensées* one of the reasons adduced why God has instituted the practice of prayer is: "Pour nous apprendre de qui nous tenons la vertu." L. 930; B. 513.

These two fragments stand in sharp contrast with the extracts quoted earlier where virtue was declared a natural attribute.[49] They also cut away the ground from under much that is claimed for Epictetus in the *Entretien*, and in particular the approval of the aim, there alleged to inform all his teaching, to bring man to consider God as his principal end.[50] For Pascal does not merely argue here that because of his infected will man requires supernatural help to supplement his own moral efforts if he is to advance along the path toward the goal marked out for him. He denies, in fact, that man can discern by natural light that God is his end, the goal wherein his nature will find the fulfilment it longs after.

The dualism which characterizes Pascal's estimate of natural ethics shows how the doctrine of the three orders determines his approach to moral questions. Taken by itself conduct based on the natural light of reason is judged virtuous, and is distinguished from wrong action or vice. But when considered in the light of the supernatural order all natural behaviour appears uniform, so that differences between virtue and vice on the natural plane disappear. Failure to appreciate this aspect of Pascal's thought explains Professor Demorest's attempt to make out a case for "honnêteté" as the stepping-stone to faith in Pascal's moral scheme.[51] To interpret "honnêteté" in this way, as the threshold of faith, is to disregard completely the doctrine of the orders, as it rules out the possibility of any such bridges from the natural order, where "honnêteté" rightly belongs, to the supernatural.

Nor does M. Demorest's contention, that according to Pascal "l'honnête homme est un chrétien en puissance",[52] advance his thesis. For it follows from Pascal's conception of the inscrutable character of divine election that every other person has equal potential for this.[53] And M. Demorest fails to bring evidence to show that Pascal considers the "honnête homme" a more likely candidate to receive the gift of grace than any other man. Besides, the infinite gulf which he fixes between the natural and supernatural orders makes differences on the purely human and natural level appear to Pascal as of no account when looked at from the standpoint of the supernatural order.

M. Demorest sees Pascal as a follower of Montaigne, Du Vair and

---

[49] Cf. above p. 19.

[50] C. p. 562; G.E. IV, p. 32.

[51] J. J. Demorest, *L'honnête homme et le croyant selon Pascal, Modern Philology*, vol. 53, no. 4, 1956, pp. 217-226. Cf. also J. Morel, *Réflexions sur le 'sentiment' pascalien, Revue des sciences humaines*, 1960, p. 26.

[52] Art. cit., p. 218.

[53] Cf. L. 427; B. 194, and 5th letter to Mlle de Roannez, C. p. 512; G.E. VI, p. 162.

Guez de Balzac, presenting the ancient philosophers in the guise of "honnêtes hommes" and so as pre-Christians. In support of this view he cites some lines from the *Pensées*.

On ne s'imagine Platon et Aristote qu'avec de grandes robes de pédants. C'étaient des gens honnêtes . . .[54]

But this interpretation takes no account of the numerous passages in Pascal's works reflecting a harsh attitude toward the virtuous pagans,[55] nor of the unfavourable comparisons which he makes on several occasions between the moral philosophy taught by the ancient philosophers and the sort of conduct inspired in the early Christians by the Holy Spirit.[56] When read in the light of such passages the extract in question serves rather to illustrate the gulf dividing the mere "honnête homme" from the Christian.[57]

   M. Demorest also seems to have overlooked the important passage at the end of the *Trois discours sur la condition des grands,* after Pascal has completed his advice to the future duke as to how best to use the privileges and discharge the duties of his office. Pascal goes on to say that even though following out this line of conduct will not suffice to save him from perdition, at least he will damn himself as an "honnête homme", and not because of brutality, avarice or debauchery. But although the alternative which he offers is more in accordance with "honnêteté", Pascal emphasizes that to damn oneself is always foolish. In order to escape this uninviting end

Il faut mépriser la concupiscence et son royaume, et aspirer à ce royaume de charité où tous les sujets ne respirent que la charité, et ne désirent que les biens de la charité.[58]

The full significance of this last statement becomes clear when it is recalled that Pascal's advice to his young pupil, which if applied will make him an "honnête homme", is directed toward his future status of "roi de concupiscence".[59] The evidence here therefore can hardly be

---

[54] L. 533; B. 331. Demorest, art. cit., p. 218.
[55] Cf. L. 691; B. 432. L. 140; B. 466. L. 923; B. 905. L. 359; B. 481.
[56] Cf. L. 338; B. 724. L. 301; B. 772, and letter to Monsieur et Madame Périer, 17th October, 1651, C. p. 492; G.E. II, pp. 540-1.
[57] M. Magendie quotes the two passages from the *Pensées* where Pascal specifically contrasts mere "honnêteté" with Christian morality (L. 426; B. 542. L. 427; B. 194) as evidence that "Il mettait la foi bien au-dessus de l'honnêteté, . . ." *La politesse mondaine et les théories de l'honnêteté, en France, au XVIIe siècle, de 1600 à 1660,* Paris 1925, p. 828.
[58] C. pp. 620-1; G.E. IX, p. 373.
[59] C. p. 620; G.E. IX, p. 372.

said to favour any interpretation of the "honnête homme" as a Christian in embryo, nor does "honnêteté" appear to carry any assurance of preferential treatment on judgement-day.

There is an interesting contrast between Pascal's views on this point and those of his fellow Port-Royalist Nicole. The estimate of "honnêteté", which M. Demorest attributes without justification to Pascal, is precisely the one formed in the *Essais de morale*. Since the Fall men have become basically anti-social by nature, but Nicole believes that reason encouraging enlightened "amour-propre" will produce a polity mirroring charity. It is important especially for tutors of the nobility to bear this in mind, so that even if they fail to inspire "sentimens de charité" in their pupils, they may at least try to tailor their "amour-propre" by showing that the means normally used to satisfy it are false and contrary to their true interest. The tutor's function is to point out how easy it is to choose other means which lead without difficulty to honour and glory, and bring universal affection, esteem and admiration.

S'ils ne réüssissoient pas par ce moyen à les rendre utiles à eux-mêmes, ils réüssiroient au-moins à les rendre utiles aux autres, et ils les mettroient dans un chemin qui seroit toujours moins éloigné de la voie du Ciel, que celui qu'ils prennent; puisqu'ils n'auroient presque qu'à changer de fin et d'intention, pour se rendre aussi agréables à Dieu par une vertu vraiment chrétienne, qu'ils le seroient aux hommes par l'éclat de cette honnêteté humaine à laquelle on les formeroit.[60]

Nicole goes further here than in most other contexts where he sets out to show that enlightened "amour-propre" may produce results that will mirror charity, and further than the title of this chapter implies, that enlightened "amour-propre" can correct social blemishes.[61] Marcel Raymond fails to do full justice to his attitude when he claims that in the *Traité de la charité et de l'amour-propre* "honnêteté" amounts only to "une parodie de la charité".[62] Unlike Pascal, Nicole is prepared to ascribe value to "honnêteté" looked at even from the supernatural point of view. And in this context at least it is clear that for him the terms "fin" and "intention" have a quite different bearing on morals from that given to them by Pascal.

---

[60] *Essais de morale,* vol. III, Paris 1755, p. 182.
[61] *De la charité et de l'amour-propre. Chapitre XI. L'amour-propre éclairé pourroit corriger tous les défauts extérieurs du monde, et former une société très-réglée.*
[62] *Du jansénisme à la morale de l'intérêt, Mercure de France,* no. 1126, 1957, p. 243.

2. THE *PROVINCIALES*

Pascal's dualistic approach to natural ethics is apparent also in the *Provinciales*. He refers there on occasion to nature as the criterion of morals. When he denounces the Jesuit casuists at the beginning of the fourteenth letter for their decisions about homicide he implies that divine law and the law of reason, which is imprinted in men's natures, coincide.

... vous êtes éloignés des sentiments de l'Eglise, et même de la nature.... vous avez tellement oublié la loi de Dieu, et tellement éteint les lumières naturelles, que vous avez besoin qu'on vous remette dans les principes les plus simples de la religion et du sens commun; car qu'y a-t-il de plus naturel que ce sentiment: 'Qu'un particulier n'a pas droit sur la vie d'un autre'?

Pascal then goes on to appeal to the authority of Saint Chrysostom in support of the view that men know how they ought to act in a situation like this by natural insight.

Nous en sommes tellement instruits de nous-mêmes,... que, quand Dieu a établi le précepte de ne point tuer, il n'a pas ajouté que c'est à cause que l'homicide est un mal; parce, dit ce Père, que la loi suppose qu'on a déjà appris cette vérité de la nature.[63]

If Christian moral precepts presuppose a knowledge of such natural truths, as that homicide is evil, then clearly these basic principles of common sense, as Pascal also calls them, form a kind of moral groundwork. The more specifically Christian code of behaviour turns out to be based on knowledge derived from natural moral insight, so that Pascal can be said to echo in this context the scholastic tenet that the natural light of reason is the basis of conduct.[64]

The obvious "moral earnestness" [65] of the *Provinciales* also has led some commentators to the conclusion that the real purpose of the work is to uphold the validity of man's natural moral insight as the guide to right and wrong. They believe that throughout the *Provinciales* Pascal appeals continually to the conscience when he denounces Jesuit practices, and that his whole case against the Jesuits depends upon establishing the fact that their principles run counter to the dictates of conscience.[66]

---

[63] C. p. 819; G.E. VI, pp. 130-1. Cf. C. p. 826; G.E. VI, p. 145.
[64] Cf. Saint Thomas Aquinas, *Summa Theologica*, Ia IIae, Q. 19, a.4; Q. 91, a.2; E. Gilson, *L'esprit de la philosophie médiévale*, 2nd ed., Paris 1944, pp. 316-8, and A.-D. Sertillanges, *La philosophie morale de Saint Thomas D'Aquin*, Paris 1916, pp. 127-148.
[65] G. N. Clark, *The Seventeenth Century*, 2nd. ed., Oxford 1947, p. 314.
[66] M. Pellisson, in an article entitled: *La sécularisation de la morale au XVIIIe siècle*, maintains, "Quand Pascal intenta aux jésuites le grand procès, où il dénonce

Now although the term conscience occurs frequently in the *Provinciales,* apparently with its usual meaning,[67] Pascal makes no express appeal to it as man's natural guide to conduct. Indeed the precise function which he assigns to it is rather difficult to determine. While discussing Lessius's opinion, that the right of self-defence covers all that is necessary to preserve oneself from any hurt, Pascal points out that it is in the interests especially of those holding public office to oppose such views, which would expose them to attacks from intending rebels who

... n'auront plus à vaincre les remords de la conscience, qui arrêtent la plupart des crimes dans leur naissance, et ne penseront plus qu'à surmonter les obstacles du dehors.[68]

In the fifteenth letter, commenting on the Jesuit maxim that it is "probable et sûr en conscience qu'on peut calomnier sans crime pour conserver son honneur," Pascal remarks that

les restrictions mentales, ... ce n'est pas au tribunal de l'Eglise qu'il cite ses adversaires; c'est à la conscience qu'il en appelle. Il sent qu'en pareille cause il n'appartient à aucune religion de rendre la sentence; et, à cette heure, pélagien inconscient, il met son suprême recours dans cette morale qui, comme eût dit Montaigne, a été plantée au cœur même de l'homme." *La révolution française,* 1903, p. 397. In a similar vein, in his article *La transformation des idées morales et la naissance des morales rationnelles de 1680 à 1715,* G. Lanson writes, "Bayle fut le premier qui démontra le principe de la souveraineté de la conscience. Mais ce principe existait déjà ... C'est en y faisant appel que Pascal pouvait rendre ridicule le jésuite qui parlait d'après la conscience du P. Bauny, et non d'après la sienne." *Revue du mois,* IX, 1910, pp. 18-19.

[67] "Vous êtes obligés en conscience, ... de dire ..." C. p. 679; G.E. IV, p. 165. "dites-moi, en conscience, ... Vous parlez donc, ... contre votre conscience? Point du tout, dit-il: je ne parlais pas en cela selon ma conscience, mais selon celle de Ponce et du Père Bauny." C. p. 709; G.E. IV, p. 309. "La plaisante comparaison, .. des choses du monde à celles de la conscience!" C. p. 710; G.E. IV, p. 311. "Et ainsi, ... un seul docteur peut tourner les consciences et les bouleverser à son gré, ..." C. *ibid.;* G. E. IV, p. 310. "... vous avez bien mis ceux qui suivent vos opinions probables en assurance à l'égard de Dieu et de la conscience; ..." C. p. 726; G.E. V, p. 50. "... les cas de conscience ..." C. *ibid.;* G.E.V, p. 51 "C'est par cette subtilité de conscience qu'il a prouvé ..." C. pp. 802-3; G.E. V, p. 382. "Je vous demande donc si cette maxime d'Escobar peut être suivie en conscience..." C. p. 804; G.E.V, p. 386. "Quand vous avez entrepris de décider les cas de conscience d'une manière favorable et accommodante, ..." C. p. 810; G.E. VI, p. 28. "... les questions de la contrition, ... qui ne touchent que l'intérieur des consciences." *ibid.* "... en leur déclarant qu'ils le peuvent faire en sûreté de conscience, ..." C. p. 816; G.E. VI, p. 39. "... je ne puis sortir [de l'hérésie], ou qu'en trahissant ma conscience, ou qu'en réformant la vôtre." C. p. 839; G.E. VI, p. 198.

[68] C. p. 826; G.E. VI, p. 144.

L'inclination corrompue des hommes s'y porte d'elle-même avec tant d'impétuo-
sité qu'il est incroyable qu'en levant l'obstacle de la conscience, elle ne se répande
avec toute sa véhémence naturelle.[69]

Despite appearances Pascal is not simply claiming here that because of
their "inclination corrompue" men are not disposed to do what their
conscience spontaneously recognizes that they ought to do, and that it
is further weakened because the Jesuits are on the side of these inclinations. No appeal at all is made to the authority of conscience. Yet
if Pascal does look to it as a clear and reliable guide on moral questions
he must, to be consistent, show it as rejecting Jesuit principles which
flatly contradict its judgements. The contradiction is plain enough. It is
precisely the authority of conscience which is lacking. The need in which
it stands of guidance explains Pascal's concern to expose the morally
pernicious effects of the Jesuit principles. Its voice is silenced by the
weight of Jesuit assurances, and it requires to have the main lines of
what is right and what is wrong clearly pointed out before it can exercise
its sanctioning function.[70]

A further passage from a later fragment, criticizing the Jesuit approach
to the problems of moral theology, shows just how far Pascal is from
relying on the conscience by itself to find out what is right and what is
wrong.

Les Jésuites ont voulu joindre Dieu au monde et n'ont gagné que le mépris de
Dieu et du monde. Car du côté de la conscience cela est évident, et du côté du
monde...[71]

The fragment implies quite definitely that the proper rule of conscience
is the will of God; so that if Pascal can be said to insist on the primacy
of the conscience it is always a conscience instructed and guided by the
precepts set out in Scripture.

The conscience, therefore, is not in Pascal's view a source of independent moral judgement at all. It is not by the exercise of conscience
that men determine what is good or bad in conduct. For the individual
to be able to discern the moral quality of intentions or actions, and to
see where duty lies, Pascal believes that he must know the will of God.
The office of the conscience consists simply in applying to a given
situation a ready-made code of right and wrong. As Pascal describes it

---

[69] C. p. 835; G.E. VI, p. 191.
[70] Cf. from the *Pensées:* "En montrant la vérité, on la fait croire;... On assure
la conscience en montrant la fausseté;..." L. 847; B. 893. "Jamais on ne fait le
mal si pleinement et si gaiement que quand on le fait par conscience." L. 813;
B. 895.
[71] L. 989; B. 935.

in operation the conscience seems to include no more than the individual's awareness that he is or is not doing what has been marked out as right by God's will revealed in Scripture.

Moreover, the claim that Pascal appeals constantly in the *Provinciales* to the conscience in order to ascertain the morality of the Jesuit position overlooks one of his favourite devices for holding the Jesuits up to derision. This consists in showing that their innovations have had the effect of aligning Christian with natural morality, and that as a result theirs is a purely pagan ethic. In the fifth letter Pascal's Jansenist alleges that this confusion of the Christian and pagan moral points of view underlies the errors in the Jesuit doctrine of grace.

Comme leur morale est toute païenne, la nature suffit pour l'observer. Quand nous soutenons la nécessité de la grâce efficace, nous lui donnons d'autres vertus pour objet.... c'est pour une vertu plus haute que celle des pharisiens et des plus sages du paganisme. La loi et la raison sont des grâces suffisantes pour ces effets. Mais pour dégager l'âme de l'amour du monde, pour la retirer de ce qu'elle a de plus cher, ... ce n'est l'ouvrage que d'une main toute-puissante. Et il est aussi peu raisonnable de prétendre que l'on a toujours un plein pouvoir, qu'il le serait de nier que ces vertus, destituées d'amour de Dieu, lesquelles ces bons Pères confondent avec les vertus chrétiennes, ne sont pas en notre puissance.[72]

Pascal is not concerned therefore to deny the possibility of a pagan ethic which aims at producing virtues wholly within the range of man's natural capacity. It is his object rather to mark the sharp distinction between such an ethic and what he considers the true Christian conception of morality. By equating the Jesuit system with pagan morality he intends to emphasize just how far it diverges from the Christian tradition.

The same distinction is underlined in the fourth letter where the Jansenist objects to the Jesuit tenet that no one sins without prior knowledge of his 'infirmity' and 'physician', nor without having previously experienced the desire to be cured and to implore God to that end.

---

[72] C. p. 707; G.E. IV, p. 304. This radical disparity between the range of man's natural power and that of divine grace for "vertu," is insisted on in the *Pensées* also. In a fragment devoted to showing how the Old Testament predictions were fulfilled, Pascal claims: "... il est arrivé qu'en la quatrième monarchie, ... les païens en foule adorent Dieu et mènent une vie angélique; ... les hommes renoncent à tous plaisirs. Ce que Platon n'a pu persuader à quelque peu d'hommes choisis et si instruits, une force secrète le persuade à cent millions d'hommes ignorants, ... Qu'est-ce que tout cela? C'est l'esprit de Dieu qui est répandu sur la terre." L. 338; B. 724. In another fragment he notes: "La conversion des païens n'était réservée qu'à la grâce du Messie. Les Juifs ont été si longtemps à les combattre sans succès: ... Les sages comme Platon et Socrate, n'ont pu le persuader." L. 447; B. 769.

Pensera-t-on que ces philosophes, qui vantaient si hautement la puissance de la nature, en connussent l'infirmité et le médecin? Direz-vous que ceux qui soutenaient, comme une maxime assurée, 'que ce n'est pas Dieu qui donne la vertu, et qu'il ne s'est jamais trouvé personne qui la lui ait demandée', pensassent à la lui demander eux-mêmes? [73]

This extract, in its context, shows quite plainly Pascal's opinion of the sort of ethical theory which treats nature as by itself capable of motivating and effecting virtuous acts, and which has as its object a virtue whose source is not in some God-given movement of the heart.

The opening paragraphs of the *Factum pour les curés de Paris* are notable for an even more outspoken attack on natural morality, when Pascal claims that the whole aim of Jesuit moral theology is to accommodate Christ's teaching to the demands of human nature, instead of to raise the standard of human life to conform to that teaching.[74] If the Jesuits have their way, Pascal maintains, men will end by relying solely on the natural light of reason as their guide to the principles of action, and the law of God will be annihilated.[75]

This substitution of human for divine authority in ethics, which results from the Jesuits' corrupting influence, is again deplored in the *Second écrit des curés de Paris*, when Pascal alleges that their 'detestable moral teaching' consists in setting up

... leurs traditions humaines sur la ruine des traditions divines.[76]

The gulf which separates these two types of morality, despite what may appear to be superficial resemblances, is effectively brought out in a figurative passage from some notes obviously intended for the *Provinciales*.

Un bâtiment également beau par dehors, mais sur un mauvais fondement. Les païens sages le bâtissaient; et le diable trompe les hommes par cette ressemblance apparente fondée sur le fondement le plus différent.[77]

---

[73] C. p. 697; G.E. IV, pp. 258-9. Cf. C. p. 774; G.E. V, p. 267, and H. F. Stewart, *Les Provinciales de Blaise Pascal*, Manchester 1920, p. 292 (note to p. 114, 1.37). In the *Cinquième écrit des curés de Paris* Pascal maintains that although schism represents a much more serious evil than the moral laxity encouraged by Jesuit casuistry, this evil "est néanmoins plus dangereux, en ce qu'il est plus conforme aux sentiments de la nature, et que les hommes y ont d'eux-mêmes une telle inclination qu'il est besoin d'une vigilance continuelle pour les en garder." C. p. 938, G.E. VII, p. 373. Cf. *Factum pour les curés de Paris*, C. p. 917; G.E. VII, p. 298.
[74] C. pp. 907-8; G.E. VII, p. 280.
[75] C. p. 913; G.E. VII, pp. 290-1.
[76] C. p. 923; G.E. VII, p. 318.
[77] L. 960; B. 921. Cf. L. 985; B. 942. Pascal follows Saint Augustine when he insists here that the resemblances between pagan and Christian morality are merely apparent, so that the moral quality of outwardly similar acts is radically

Once again the contrast is worked in to discredit Jesuit moral theology by showing that it is based upon natural principles. The extract implies that such virtues as pagan ethical teaching may produce, when judged by the Christian criterion, will not be seen as real virtues at all.

An admirable summary of Pascal's views on this question is set out in a passage from a fragment usually included in the *Pensées*, but clearly written with the Jesuits very much in mind.

Toutes les religions et les sectes du monde ont eu la raison naturelle pour guide. Les seuls chrétiens ont été astreints à prendre leurs règles hors d'eux-mêmes, et à s'informer de celles que Jésus-Christ a laissées aux anciens pour être retransmises aux fidèles. Cette contrainte lasse ces bons Pères. Ils veulent avoir, comme les autres peuples, la liberté de suivre leurs imaginations.[78]

It is interesting to note that in an earlier variant of this fragment, afterwards deleted, Pascal wrote

Ils ont dit aux peuples: 'Venez à nous; nous suivrons les opinions des nouveaux auteurs; la raison sera notre guide; nous serons comme les autres peuples qui suivent chacun sa lumière naturelle.' [79]

Since the principles of Jesuit moral theology, which Pascal wishes to disparage, are treated as indistinguishable from those of any secular or pagan morality, whereas the Christian ethic is superior because it is not based on nature,[80] it is quite plain what estimate Pascal forms of natural morality. And the readiness which he asserts the Christian should show to allow the religious tradition to mould his ethical judgements denies the competence of the natural light of reason for that purpose.

This claim, that there is a religious tradition, embodied in Scripture and in the writings of the Fathers and the canons of the Church, which is the guide to true Christian morality, is a constantly recurring one in the *Provinciales* and the *Pensées*.[81] And it is clear that it is the divergence

different. N. P. Williams summarizes Saint Augustine's views on this point as follows: "Pagans ... being incapable of receiving grace, cannot perform any really good or meritorious work at all: their apparent virtues are merely 'splendid vices' ... and all the morality of a Socrates or a Cato is merely a hollow show." *The Grace of God*, London 1930, pp. 23-4. Cf. E. Gilson, *Introduction à l'étude de Saint Augustin*, p. 198, n.l.

[78] L. 769; B. 903.

[79] L. *ibid.*; B. 903 bis.

[80] Cf. also from the *Pensées:* "La seule religion contre la nature, contre le sens commun, contre nos plaisirs, est la seule qui ait toujours été." L. 284; B. 605.

[81] "... je me moque de ces auteurs-là, s'ils sont contraires à la tradition." C. p. 693; G.E. IV, p. 252. "Je croyais ne devoir prendre pour règle que l'Ecriture et la tradition de l'Eglise, mais non pas vos casuistes." C. p. 709; G.E. IV, p. 309. "C'est-à-dire, mon Père, qu'à votre arrivée on a vu disparaître saint Augustin, saint Chrysostome, ... et les autres, pour ce qui est de la morale." C. p. 713;

of Jesuit propositions from this Christian tradition which provokes
Pascal's reaction to them. The Jesuit position is not denounced in the
abstract, but always in relation to what Pascal regards as the true
Christian position; and the office of the conscience is in effect reduced
to registering disapproval at the deviation shown. Pascal's dominant
concern throughout the *Provinciales* is clearly, therefore, not to uphold
the autonomy of natural morality, but to reassert the primacy of the
Christian ethic as he sees it.

The essentially polemical nature of the *Provinciales* makes it difficult
to ascertain precisely what characterizes this ethic as against what Pascal
claims is the Jesuits' modified version of it. There are references to "les
règles les plus saintes de la conduite chrétienne . . .",[82] "les saintes règles
de l'Evangile . . .",[83] "les règles de la morale [de l'Eglise] . . .,[84] "les
règles évangéliques . . .," [85] but Pascal does not define these. There is
considerable truth in Vinet's assessment of the *Provinciales* as a treatise
on ethics: "A proprement parler, ce n'en est pas un. Non seulement
l'auteur n'apporte sur ce sujet aucun nouveau système, mais rarement il
s'engage dans l'exposition des idées reçues." [86] When he attacks the
Jesuit casuistical practices, for example, as debasing moral standards
and destroying all principles of right action, Pascal takes for granted in
his reader an acquaintance with the basic moral tenets of Christianity.
Confident that it will suffice his purpose to expose such practices in a
clear light, he is content, having done so, simply to affirm that they entail

---

G.E. IV, p. 317. ". . . je prévois . . . de puissantes barrières qui s'opposeront à
votre course. . . . l'Ecriture sainte, les papes et les Conciles . . . qui sont dans la
voie unique de l'Evangile." C. p. 714; G.E. IV, p. 319. "O mon Père! d'où Molina
a-t-il pu être éclairé pour déterminer une chose de cette importance, sans aucun
secours de l'Ecriture, des Conciles, ni des Pères?" C. p. 737; G.E. V, p. 104.
"Saint Augustin en a le plus, . . . Outre une chose qu'on peut considérer, qui est
une tradition sans interruption de 12,000 papes, conciles, etc." L. 954; B. 925.
"*Aquavivae*. Ep. XVI. Lire les Pères pour les conformer à son imagination, au
lieu de former sa pensée sur celle des Pères." L. 953; B. 958. "Il y a contradiction, car d'un côté ils disent qu'il faut suivre la tradition et n'oseraient désavouer
cela, et de l'autre ils diront ce qu'il leur plaira. On croira toujours ce premier, . . ."
L. 714; B. 944. "Je ne crains pas même vos censures, paroles si elles ne sont fondées sur celles de la tradition." L. 916; B. 920. Arnauld applies the same test of
conformity to tradition in order to determine the validity of propositions in moral
theology. Cf. J. Laporte, *La doctrine de Port-Royal*, vol. III, *La morale d'après
Arnauld*, Paris 1951, pp. 41-2.
   [82] C. p. 778; G.E. V, p. 273.
   [83] C. p. 798; G.E. V, p. 373.
   [84] C. p. 907; G.E. VII, pp. 279-280.
   [85] C. p. 915; G.E. VII, p. 295.
   [86] A. Vinet, *Etudes sur Blaise Pascal*, 5th ed., Lausanne 1936, p. 255. Pascal's
detailed treatment of the question of homicide in the 14th *Provinciale* is an exception to this general pattern.

a "renversement" of, or an "égarement" from, the Christian ethic without specifying in detail what this is. It is as if he believes the inconsistency is too glaring to need being underlined, and that labouring the point might detract from the force of his argument.[87]

[87] Even the resounding manifesto with which the *Factum pour les curés de Paris* opens is not followed by any exposition: "Notre cause est la cause de la morale chrétienne. Nos parties sont les casuistes qui la corrompent." C. p. 906; G.E. VII, p. 278. One recent commentator on the *Provinciales* claims that "the positions [Pascal] chose to attack indicate clearly enough what he himself stood for." A. J. Krailsheimer, *Studies in Self-Interest,* Oxford 1962, p. 99. It is obviously possible to infer by this indirect means that Pascal stands for the Gospel precepts in their undiluted form, and, as Antoine Adam puts it, that "Toute la critique de Pascal sous-entend que l'amour de Dieu est l'unique maxime de la morale." *Histoire de la littérature française au XVIIe siècle,* Paris 1951, vol. II, p. 253. This is backed by explicit assertions on Pascal's part: "On viole 'le grand commandement, qui comprend la loi et les prophètes'; on attaque la piété dans le cœur; on en ôte l'esprit qui donne la vie; on dit que l'amour de Dieu n'est pas nécessaire au salut;..." C. p. 778; G.E. V, p. 274. "... vous anéantissez a morale chrétienne en la séparant de l'amour de Dieu,..." C. p. 868; G.E. VI, p. 345.

CHAPTER III

PASCAL'S AUTHORITARIAN APPROACH TO ETHICS IN THE *PROVINCIALES*

It is Pascal's authoritarian approach to ethics in the *Provinciales* which determines in large part his uncompromising rejection of Jesuit moral theology and virtual surrender of the critical office of the conscience.[1] He clearly regards the moral injunctions implicit in the Christian faith as forming part of what he believes is a revealed system of truth. Two factors contributing to this authoritarian approach are his conception of theology, the discipline which in his opinion properly concerns itself with revealed truth, and his estimate of human nature.

The influence of Pascal's pessimistic view of human nature on his attitude to Jesuit moral theology comes out in a significant passage from the *Factum pour les curés de Paris*.[2] He there alleges that Jesuit casuistry amounts to a complete reversal of the groundwork of Christian ethics, which is essentially oriented to the task of raising human motives to a different plane in order that they may measure up to divine standards. Casuistry as practised by the Jesuits on the other hand involves the attempt to achieve exactly the opposite – to water down those standards so that they become more practical from the human point of view, and more compatible with human nature as it actually is.[3] Such a re-

---

[1] M. Brunschvicg, in the introduction to the *Provinciales* in the Grands Ecrivains edition, cites numerous examples to show how the Jesuit replies to the letters completely miss the mark. The main reason for this lies in the Jesuits' failure to comprehend that, after joining battle over a question of moral theology, Pascal should refuse to debate the issue according to the juristic conceptions with which the subject had become overlaid in the course of a long and almost exclusive association with the scholastic tradition. Cf. G.E. IV, pp. XXXVIII-LII.

[2] C. pp. 907-8; G.E. VII, p. 280.

[3] There is a companion fragment to this passage in the *Pensées*, where Pascal again maintains that the Jesuits' method of compromise lays axe to the very roots of Christian ethics by introducing modifications to the revealed precepts. "Ceux qui aiment l'Eglise se plaignent de voir corrompre les mœurs; mais au moins les lois subsistent. Mais ceux-ci corrompent les lois: le modèle est gâté." L. 679; B. 894.

versal of the fundamental direction of Christian ethics results in confusion of its true principle and aim. Man sets up his own reason as the yard-stick to which moral choices are referred, and looks to the gratification of his sensual appetites and passions as the goal of his every act.

Now although the context shows that even here it is his reverence for what 'tradition' leads him to regard as revealed authority which has most weight in swinging Pascal's preference so decidedly away from the Jesuit position, his low opinion of human nature plays at least a contributory role. For two paragraphs earlier, justifying his allegation that the Jesuits are exercising a particularly pernicious influence by corrupting the "règle des mœurs" through their perversion of scriptural laws, he writes:

> ... comme la nature de l'homme tend toujours au mal dès sa naissance, et qu'elle n'est ordinairement retenue que par la crainte de la loi, aussitôt que cette barrière est ôtée, la concupiscence se répand sans obstacle, de sorte qu'il n'y a point de différence entre rendre les vices permis, et rendre tous les hommes vicieux.[4]

Such a gloomy view would by itself be sufficient reason for turning to a revealed authority in ethics. Small wonder then that Pascal refuses to take any account, at least on the positive side, of the tendencies of human nature, or to concede any part to reason, where moral principles are concerned.

Another passage from the *Factum,* after some examples of the way in which the Jesuits do convert ethics into an entirely human affair, elevating reason into the criterion, further illustrates the extent to which Pascal's estimate of human nature influences his outlook.

> On voit en ce peu de mots l'esprit de ces casuistes, et comme en détruisant les règles de la piété ils font succéder aux préceptes de l'Ecriture qui nous oblige de rapporter toutes nos actions à Dieu, une permission brutale de les rapporter toutes à nous-mêmes; ...[5]

The words "permission brutale" show plainly enough the light in which Pascal sees this reversal of criteria. And that his opposition stems at least in part from an unfavourable view of human nature in its present state is made clear in the latter part of the sentence.[6] The only apparent reason why man cannot determine the morality of his own acts is that his power of ethical judgement has been warped through the corruption of his nature. By contrast, the primary assumption underlying the Jesuit

---

[4] C. p. 907; G.E. VII, p. 279.

[5] C. p. 908; G.E. VII, pp. 281-2.

[6] "... c'est-à-dire qu'au lieu que Jésus-Christ est venu pour amortir en nous les concupiscences du vieil homme et y faire régner la charité de l'homme nouveau, ceux-ci sont venus pour faire revivre les concupiscences..." C. p. 908; G.E. VII, p. 282.

moral theology, at least as Pascal sees it, is that man's reason is a competent guide on ethical questions.[7]

The other and perhaps more decisive factor combining to make him set his face against the Jesuit approach is his conception of theology as a discipline. In this respect the attack on the Jesuit casuistry in the *Provinciales* amounts to little more than putting into effect the principles stated some nine years previously in the *Préface pour le traité du vide*. Pascal there draws a sharp distinction between the 'sciences', where reason and observation must be left unhampered if knowledge is to expand, and those subjects like history, geography and jurisprudence, where what he calls 'authority' is alone capable of adding to our knowledge. In order to find out, for example, who was the first king of the French, or what words were used in a dead language, he maintains that it is necessary to refer to written records, and that knowledge on these points cannot extend beyond the information which they contain.

C'est l'autorité seule qui nous en peut éclaircir. Mais où cette autorité a la principale force, c'est dans la théologie, parce qu'elle y est inséparable de la vérité, et que nous ne la connaissons que par elle ... parce que ses principes sont au-dessus de la nature et de la raison, ...[8]

The source of authority for theology is Scripture. Further on in the *Préface* he emphasizes the "malice" of those who rely solely on reason in theology instead of looking to the authority of Scripture and the Fathers, and notes that it will be necessary to confound the insolence of those rash enough to introduce novelties in theology.[9] This clearly

---

[7] The implications of this for Pascal's assessment of casuistry are strikingly brought out in the following fragment: "Les casuistes soumettent la décision à la raison corrompue et le choix des décisions à la volonté corrompue, afin que tout ce qu'il y a de corrompu dans la nature de l'homme ait part à sa conduite. L. 601; B. 907.

[8] C. p. 530; G.E. II, p. 131. A similar distinction had already been drawn by Jansenius in his *Augustinus*, t. II, Liber Prooemialis, cap. IV, Louvain 1640, Frankfurt/Main 1964, pp. 7-10.

[9] C. p. 531; G.E. II, p. 133. Pascal simply reaffirms here the break-away from the traditional scholastic view of the nature and scope of philosophy and theology made by Jansenius. In terms of the debate, therefore, it is the 'order of sciences,' which Pascal maintains is 'perverted' by the abuses he attacks, that represents the novelty challenging accepted theological practice. According to Nicole, in his introduction to the Latin translation of the *Provinciales*, it was Pascal's declared aim in that work to adopt a fresh approach to theology, in both method and terminology, at the expense of the established scholastic tradition: "Il croioit pouvoir traiter ces questions, qui faisoient alors tant de bruit, et les débarrasser des termes obscurs et équivoques des scolastiques, des vaines chicanes de mots, ... Il esperoit, dis-je, les expliquer d'une maniere si aisée et si proportionnée à l'intelligence de tout le monde, qu'il pourroit forcer les Jésuites mêmes de se rendre à la vérité." G.E. VII, p. 68. Pascal's own remarks in the 12th letter endorse this view: "...quoique vous ayez pensé qu'en embrouillant les questions par des termes

foreshadows the attitude of the *Provinciales*. And Pascal sums up his own view in a short categorical assertion:

> ... les inventions nouvelles sont infailliblement des erreurs dans les matières que l'on profane impunément; ...[10]

The same distinction reappears in a slightly different form in the eighteenth *Provinciale*. In the course of refuting the Jesuit claim to have discovered heretical statements in Jansenius's writings Pascal outlines three principles of knowledge, the senses, reason and faith. Each of these has its own particular field of operation where it is capable of attaining certain knowledge. This means that the preliminary step in examining any proposition must always be to determine its nature in order to ascertain to which of the three principles it should be referred.

> S'il s'agit d'une chose surnaturelle, nous n'en jugerons ni par les sens, ni par la raison, mais par l'Ecriture et par les décisions de l'Eglise. S'il s'agit d'une proposition non révélée, et proportionnée à la raison naturelle, elle en sera le propre juge.[11]

It is plain, both from this passage and from the previous paragraph where he couples together "choses surnaturelles et révélées," that in Pascal's vocabulary the adjectives supernatural and revealed, if they do not denote precisely the same thing, are used at least to qualify things belonging to the same category. Scripture and the decisions of the Church therefore, not reason, must be regarded as the appropriate referees where anything related to a revealed proposition is in question.

Elsewhere Pascal insists that 'tradition' is the sole reliable guide to revealed truth. Thus in the *Cinquième écrit des curés de Paris* it is claimed that:

> Comme [notre religion] est toute divine, c'est en Dieu seul qu'elle s'appuie, et n'a de doctrine que celle qu'elle a reçue de lui par le canal de la tradition qui est notre véritable règle, ... nous ne croyons aujourd'hui que les choses que nos évêques et nos pasteurs nous ont apprises, et qu'ils avaient eux-mêmes reçues de ceux qui les ont précédés ... et les premiers qui ont été envoyés par les apôtres, n'ont dit que ce qu'ils en avaient appris.[12]

---

d'Ecole, les réponses en seraient si longues, si obscures et si épineuses qu'on en perdrait goût, cela ne sera peut-être pas tout à fait ainsi; car j'essaierai de vous ennuyer le moins qu'il se peut en ce genre d'écrire.... c'est vous qui m'engagez d'entrer dans cet éclaircissement, ..." C. p. 793; G.E. V, p. 363.

[10] C. p. 531; G.E. II, p. 134.

[11] C. p. 898; G.E. VII, p. 50.

[12] C. p. 932; G.E. VII, p. 362. Cf. *Premier écrit sur la grâce*, where Pascal maintains that in order to determine the truth of the Church's 'opinion,' as against that of her opponents, "La règle que nous prendrons pour cet effet sera la tradition successive de cette doctrine depuis Jésus-Christ jusqu'à nous." C. pp. 957-8; G.E. XI, pp. 140-1.

The true Christian tradition can be traced back in a direct line to its divine source, a valuable safeguard for doctrine from aberrations like those implicit in Jesuit moral theology. A passage from a fragment usually included in the *Pensées* further illustrates this conception of the role of tradition:

> ... l'Eglise ... aujourd'hui ... a toujours la maxime supérieure de la tradition, de la créance de l'ancienne Eglise; et ainsi cette soumission et cette conformité à l'ancienne Eglise prévaut et corrige tout.[13]

In the fifth *Provinciale* the Jesuit doctrine of probable opinions is rejected because it leads to bending the rule of action prescribed by the traditional laws and decisions of the Church.

> ... comme si la foi, et la tradition qui la maintient, n'était pas toujours une et invariable dans tous les temps et dans tous les lieux; comme si c'était à la règle à se fléchir pour convenir au sujet qui doit lui être conforme; ...[14]

Because Pascal believes that the true principles of ethics form part of a system of revealed truth, he expects those who treat moral questions to observe what he considers to be the appropriate categories. The content of revelation, in his view, relates by definition to the supernatural order, which rests on divine authority not on natural reason. And in terms of the principles outlined in the passages from the *Préface pour le traité du vide,* and the eighteenth *Provinciale,* Jesuit casuistry amounts to setting up natural reason illegitimately as arbiter in matters quite beyond its compass. As a result the Jesuits have been induced to make innovations just as if moral theology were a branch of the sciences. In fact they should have confined themselves to ascertaining and relating the decisions recorded by the Church and the Fathers. This deviation by itself would have sufficed to secure Pascal's opposition. But the Jesuits have gone even further. Instead of deciding the difference between right and wrong acts in the light of Scriptural texts, they have presumed to attenuate the revealed precepts, transmitted "par le canal de la tradition", in order to bring these into line with what Pascal regards as the corrupt tendencies of human nature. That they should then defend "comme la vraie morale de l'Eglise cette morale corrompue" [15] appears to him tantamount to rejecting the true Christian ethic in its entirety.

---

[13] L. 285; B. 867. Another fragment dealing with miracles contains the significant judgement that "... la vraie source de la vérité ... est la tradition, ..." L. 865; B. 832.

[14] C. p. 706; G.E. IV, p. 303.

[15] *Second écrit des curés de Paris,* C. p. 919; G.E. VII, p. 310. For an evaluation of the approach to theological discussion upon which Pascal bases his criticisms of Jesuit moral theology see J. Miel, *Pascal and Theology,* Baltimore and London 1969, pp. 94-8.

CHAPTER IV

PASCAL'S REJECTION OF
CONTEMPORARY ARISTOCRATIC MORALITY

Behind Pascal's attack on Jesuit casuistry in the *Provinciales* lies the demand for a reversal of the moral values prized by the contemporary nobility. It is clear from a number of passages that he believes the casuistical devices used by the Jesuits are designed to make the Christian ethic more palatable to the worldly aristocracy. In the *Second écrit des curés de Paris* he remarks that the Jesuits, who form the most powerful and numerous order in the Church, are confessors to the great.[1] And some notes for the *Provinciales* contain two significant references to the Jesuits' *politics,* the word used by Pascal to describe their attempt to come to terms with the code of behaviour accepted by that class.

Politique. – Nous avons trouvé deux obstacles au dessein de soulager les hommes: l'un, des lois intérieures de l'Evangile, l'autre, des lois extérieures de l'Etat et de la religion. Les unes, nous en sommes maîtres, les autres, . . .[2]
Le monde veut naturellement une religion, mais douce. . . . On ne vit pas long-temps dans l'impiété ouverte, ni naturellement dans les grandes austérités. Une religion accommodée est propre à durer.[3]

One of the means whereby the Jesuits try to achieve their aim of a "religion douce", whose demands will not prove offensive to their aristo-

---

[1] ". . . la plus puissante Compagnie et la plus nombreuse de l'Eglise, qui gouverne les consciences presque de tous les grands, . . ." C. p. 926; G.E. VII, p. 323. The influential position held by the Jesuits in relation to the privileged classes, for whom Pascal implies they cater especially, is underlined again in two unclassified fragments. "Je suis seul contre trente mille? Point. Gardez, vous la cour, vous l'imposture; moi la vérité." L. 960; B. 921. "Il importe aux rois et aux princes d'être en estime de piété. Et pour cela, il faut qu'ils se confessent à vous." L. 909; B. 924.
[2] L. 966; B. 926.
[3] L. 952; B. 956. The sort of compromise which the Jesuits, by the nature of their mission, were set to try and effect is described by Professor Paul Bénichou as ". . . à la fois une conquête du christianisme sur la société laïque et un recul du christianisme devant les valeurs issues spontanément des conditions de la vie noble." *Morales du grand siècle,* Paris 1948, pp. 81-2.

cratic clientèle, is the doctrine of "grâce actuelle", which reduces drastic-
ally the scope of sinful acts. In the fourth letter Pascal claims that this
plays into the hands of those whose whole life is taken up with

... une recherche continuelle de toutes sortes de plaisirs, dont jamais le moindre
remords n'a interrompu le cours.[4]

And in reply to the Jesuit's attempt to get round this difficulty, by alleg-
ing that even such persons as these do experience a God-given desire to
avoid their sinful actions, Pascal objects

... je me tiens obligé ... de vous désabuser, et de vous dire qu'il y a mille gens
qui n'ont point ces désirs, qui pèchent sans regret, qui pèchent avec joie, ... Et qui
peut en savoir plus de nouvelles que vous? Il n'est pas que vous ne confessiez
quelqu'un de ceux dont je parle; car c'est parmi les personnes de grande qualité
qu'il s'en rencontre d'ordinaire.[5]

In the seventh letter Pascal maintains that the method of directing the
intention has been developed to condone the dominant passion of the
privileged classes for the point of honour, and the violent means usually
employed to vindicate it.[6] When the Jesuit describes the gulf separating
the "loi de l'Evangile", from the "lois du monde", which the casuists
believe they have managed to bridge by this principle, Pascal, with
tongue in cheek, is forced to admit that his first reaction of astonishment
at their success was not strong enough.

Je tiendrais la chose impossible, si, après ce que j'ai vu de vos Pères, je ne savais
qu'ils peuvent faire facilement ce qui est impossible aux autres hommes. C'est ce
qui me fait croire qu'ils en ont bien trouvé quelque moyen, ...[7]

The ironical reply shows that Pascal regards as utterly irreconcilable
the two terms which the Jesuits attempt to reconcile in this way, "piété"
and "honneur".

Moreover, according to him the whole doctrine of probabilism has its
roots in the desire to come to terms with current aristocratic values.

---

[4] C. p. 695; G.E. IV, p. 255.
[5] C. p. 696; G.E. IV, p. 257.
[6] By this method the casuists are allegedly able to permit "les violences qu'on
pratique en défendant son honneur. Car il n'y a qu'à détourner son intention du
désir de vengeance, qui est criminel, pour la porter au désir de défendre son
honneur, qui est permis selon nos Pères. Et c'est ainsi qu'ils accomplissent tous
leurs devoirs envers Dieu et envers les hommes." C. pp. 728-9; G.E. V, pp. 86-7.
In Pascal's terms this procedure amounts to effecting a compromise of "les lois
humaines avec les divines." ibid.
[7] C. p. 728; G.E. V, p. 85.

Que serait-ce que les Jésuites sans la probabilité, et que la probabilité sans les Jésuites? Otez la *probabilité*, on ne peut plus plaire au monde; mettez la *proba-bilité*, on ne peut plus lui déplaire.[8]

Peut-ce être autre chose que la complaisance du monde qui vous fasse trouver les choses probables? Nous ferez-vous accroire que ce soit la vérité, et que, si la mode du duel n'était point, vous trouveriez probable qu'on se peut battre, en regardant la chose en elle-même?[9]

By decreeing that any opinion which can claim the authority of even a single doctor is probable, and may therefore be followed in conscience, the Jesuits are able to expunge, or at least to play down so that they cease to obtrude, those elements in the Christian ethical system which the worldly aristocracy finds distasteful. And Pascal obviously sees Jesuit moral theology as not merely oriented toward, but in effect dictated by what is current practice among the worldly.

The design of embracing the whole world within the arms of the Christian faith, which leads the Jesuits to adopt this "conduite 'o-bligeante et accommodante' "[10] toward the code of behaviour favoured by the privileged classes, is not in itself the target for Pascal's criticism; even if he does suggest that it has its springs in self-esteem, in the desire for the advancement of their own cause rather than that of the Christian religion.[11] But he considers that, in order to realize their ideal of a

---

[8] L. 981; B. 918.

[9] L. 644; B. 910. Brunetière maintains that the Jesuits saw in probabilism "un moyen de concilier les exigences de la morale chrétienne avec le train du monde;... Les textes sont formels sur ce point: 'Combien n'ont-ils pas tort, s'écrie Escobar, dans le *Préambule* de sa grande *Théologie morale*, ceux qui se plaignent qu'en matière de conduite, les docteurs leur produisent tant et de si diverses décisions! Mais ils devraient plutôt s'en réjouir, en y voyant autant de motifs nouveaux de consolation et d'espérance. Car la diversité des opinions en morale, c'est le joug du Seigneur rendu plus facile et plus doux!...' Et il dit encore plus loin,...: 'La Providence a voulu, dans son infinie bonté, qu'il y eût plusieurs moyens de se tirer d'affaire en morale, et que les voies de la vertu fussent larges, 'patescere', afin de vérifier la parole du Psalmiste: 'Vias tuas, Domine, demonstra mihi.' Voilà le dernier terme du *probabilisme*,..." *Etudes critiques sur l'histoire de la littérature française*, Quatrième série, Paris 1898, pp. 93-4.

[10] C. p. 705; G.E. IV, p. 300.

[11] Cf. from the 5th letter: "Ils ont assez bonne opinion d'eux-mêmes pour croire qu'il est utile et comme nécessaire au bien de la religion que leur crédit s'étende partout, et qu'ils gouvernent toutes les consciences." Hence the scriptural precepts are enforced with full rigour or relaxed as the circumstances require. C. pp. 704-5; G.E., IV, pp. 299-300. In the 16th letter Pascal comments on the permission granted by numerous casuists to take communion after committing even the most abomi-nable sins: "Voilà ce que c'est, mes Pères, d'avoir des Jésuites par toute la terre. Voilà la pratique universelle que vous y avez introduite... Il n'importe que les tables de Jésus-Christ soient remplies d'abominations, pourvu que vos églises soient pleines de monde." C. p. 854; G.E. VI, p. 270. And in a brief fragment included in the *Pensées* he maintains: "Ils ne peuvent avoir la perpétuité, et ils cherchent l'universalité; et pour cela ils font toute l'Eglise corrompue, afin qu'ils soient saints." L. 707; B. 898.

Church co-extensive with the world, the Jesuits are stooping to unworthy compromises. As he sees it they try to make Christianity acceptable to the nobility by diluting its distinctive ethical content. His own insistence is that the Christian ethic requires the world to be levelled up, not the Church to be levelled down. And the reason why casuistical decisions authorizing such aristocratic pastimes as duelling should be singled out so frequently for condemnation is not simply because this represents the most vulnerable point in the Jesuit armour. It is also for the more basic reason that the aristocratic way of life requires more numerous and more serious attenuations than any other in the standard of Christian conduct prized so highly by Pascal, if the sort of compromise aimed at by the Jesuits is to be secured.

The code of values subscribed to by the great majority of Pascal's aristocratic contemporaries has been outlined by Professor Paul Béni-chou: "Dans ce qui subsistait alors de la société féodale, les valeurs suprêmes étaient l'ambition, l'audace, le succès. Le poids de l'épée, la hardiesse des appétits et du verbe faisaient le mérite; le mal résidait dans la faiblesse ou la timidité, dans le fait de désirer peu, d'oser petite-ment, de subir une blessure sans la rendre: on s'excluait par là du rang des maîtres pour rentrer dans le commun troupeau." [12] A passage from the fourteenth *Provinciale* shows that it is these values which Pascal rejects so emphatically in his attack on Jesuit casuistry. Adapting Saint Augustine's division between the "civitas Dei" and the "civitas terrena" to his own purpose, he notes that there are two peoples and two worlds spread throughout the earth. The world of God's children forms a body whose head and king is Christ, while the world which is hostile to God has the devil as its head and king. Christ, Pascal claims, has established in the Church, his empire, such laws as seemed good to him, and the devil has done likewise in the world, his kingdom.

Jésus-Christ a mis l'honneur à souffrir; le diable à ne point souffrir. Jésus-Christ a dit à ceux qui reçoivent un soufflet de tendre l'autre joue; et le diable a dit à ceux à qui on veut donner un soufflet de tuer ceux qui voudront leur faire cette injure.

[12] *Morales du grand siècle*, p. 19. In his chapter entitled "La démolition du héros", M. Bénichou shows how the Jansenist strain in seventeenth century French literature tended to undermine the 'heroic' values to which the nobility looked as their ideals in conduct. What represented for the contemporary aristocracy an ideal, was treated by the pessimistic moralists as basically vicious, the sign of man's fallen condition. Cf. A. O. Lovejoy, *op. cit.*, ch. 1-2. M. Bénichou links this attitude with a reaction against moral laxity which set in after the religious wars of the previous century. Cf. *Morales...* p. 123. Substantially the same point is made by Professor Antoine Adam in his Zaharoff Lecture, *Sur le problème religieux dans la première moitié du XVIIe siècle*, Oxford 1959, pp. 13-15.

Jésus-Christ déclare heureux ceux qui participent à son ignominie, et le diable déclare malheureux ceux qui sont dans l'ignominie. Jésus-Christ dit: Malheur à vous, quand les hommes diront du bien de vous! et le diable dit: Malheur à ceux dont le monde ne parle pas avec estime! [13]

The standards of the Church, far from being indistinguishable from those of the world, are therefore radically different. And the values which Pascal declares derive from the devil mirror those listed by Professor Bénichou. The position which Pascal adopts on this question, then, involves him in a thorough-going rejection of the whole basis of the current aristocratic code of behaviour, with which the Jesuits set themselves to effect a workable compromise from the nobility's point of view.

Earlier in the same letter Pascal takes the Jesuits to task over what he regards as their attempts to adjust the demands of the Christian moral law to those of the point of honour cherished by the nobility. He maintains that no amount of equivocation on their part can disguise the fact that their casuists make it permissible to kill in order to defend one's honour, and so authorize duels. The only authority that can be adduced in support of such diabolical precepts is a piece of what Pascal describes as "raisonnement impie".

L'honneur est plus cher que la vie. Or, il est permis de tuer pour défendre sa vie. Donc il est permis de tuer pour défendre son honneur?' Quoi! mes Pères, parce que le dérèglement des hommes leur a fait aimer ce faux honneur plus que la vie que Dieu leur a donnée pour le servir, il leur sera permis de tuer pour le conserver? C'est cela même qui est un mal horrible, d'aimer cet honneur-là, plus que la vie. Et cependant cette attache vicieuse, qui serait capable de souiller les actions les plus saintes, si on les rapportait à cette fin, . . . [14]

Despite the considerable element of clever tactics here Pascal's own attitude toward the aristocratic pratices, which the Jesuits set out to condone, is clear enough. For it is by no means just the Jesuit casuistry that comes in for denunciation in this passage. When he describes maxims which no French aristocrat of the time would have hesitated to

---

[13] Pascal goes on to point out that on this reckoning the Jesuit decisions making it permissible to kill in the event of receiving an affront, rather than to turn the other cheek, and agreeing that to let an affront go unavenged would involve loss of honour, classify their authors as "enfants du diable". C. p. 831; G.E. VI, p. 154. It is this 'honour', which they, in common with their aristocratic clientèle, show themselves so anxious to preserve unsullied, that the devil "a transmis de son esprit superbe en celui de ses superbes enfants. C'est cet honneur qui a toujours été l'idole des hommes, possédés par l'esprit du monde . . . l'honneur des Chrétiens consiste dans l'observation des ordres de Dieu et des règles du christianisme, et non pas dans ce fantôme d'honneur que vous prétendez, tout vain qu'il soit, être une excuse légitime pour les meurtres." C. pp. 831-2; G.E. VI, pp. 154-5.
[14] C. p. 825; G.E. VI, pp. 142-3.

endorse, at least in word if not in deed, as profane argument, and adherence to them as a terrible evil and a vicious attachment, which stem from human disorder, Pascal undermines the foundations of a whole body of accepted values, and sets up by contrast a criterion which would have found little favour in the eyes of the privileged classes.

The use of the term honour elsewhere, without these derogatory implications, suggests that Pascal is opposed to it as the principle determining conduct only as it is interpreted in such contexts by the worldly aristocracy. If looked to as the end in conduct this false aristocratic honour [15] suffices to contaminate even the holiest acts. But this implies that there is a true honour, which may be legitimately proposed as a criterion of action. And in the fourteenth letter Pascal actually refers to "l'honneur des Chrétiens", which prompts them to act in accordance with the divine will.[16] He contrasts it with the nobility's mere "fantôme d'honneur", which motivates such depraved practices as duelling. Again, in some notes obviously intended for the *Provinciales,* he describes the Jesuits as:

Gens sans parole, sans foi, sans honneur, sans vérité, . . .[17]

Honour here carries a positive moral value since it is set on a par with such virtues as keeping one's word and speaking the truth.[18]

In the seventh letter the account of decisions which have resulted from applying the Jesuit principle of directing the intention to concrete instances again provokes Pascal's criticism of the aristocratic point of honour that lies behind it. Commenting on the judgement of Hurtado and Escobar, that it is permissible to fight a duel in order to defend one's honour, he notes

---

[15] Cf. also the *Second écrit des curés de Paris,* where Pascal again denounces this false honour. "Nous les voyons . . . autoriser opiniâtrement la vengeance, l'avarice, la volupté, le faux honneur, . . ." C. p. 926; G.E. VII, p. 323. In the *Pensées* care for such honour is listed as a "divertissement". "*Divertissement.* – On charge les hommes, dès l'enfance, du soin de leur honneur, . . . on leur fait entendre qu'ils ne sauraient être heureux sans que . . . leur honneur . . . soit en bon état, . . ." L. 139; B. 143. Elsewhere it is described as a manifestation of that desire for the esteem of our fellows which leads us eventually to replace our real selves by the façade we wish to appear as: . . . "nous voulons vivre dans l'idée des autres d'une vie imaginaire, et nous nous efforçons pour cela de paraître . . . qui ne mourrait pour conserver son honneur, celui-là serait infâme. L. 806; B. 147.

[16] C. pp. 831-2; G.E. VI, pp. 154-5.

[17] L. 909; B. 924.

[18] In the *Cinquième écrit des curés de Paris,* Pascal alleges that in the present state of confusion, which results from the Jesuits treating as Calvinists all those not subscribing to their views while the Calvinists regard all Catholics as Jesuits, it is impossible to postpone the work of clarification "sans exposer l'honneur de l'Eglise et le salut d'une infinité de personnes." C. p. 935; G.E. VII, p. 367.

J'admirai sur ces passages de voir que la piété du roi emploie sa puissance à défendre et à abolir le duel dans ses Etats, et que la piété des Jésuites occupe leur subtilité à le permettre et à l'autoriser dans l'Eglise.[19]

And following the Jesuit's exposition of Escobar's maxim, that it is legitimate to kill in order to avenge an insult and so preserve one's honour, Pascal remarks

Cela me parut si horrible, que j'eus peine à me retenir; mais, pour savoir le reste, je le laissai continuer ainsi . . .[20]

A little further on he describes his reaction when asked by the Jesuit if he wanted additional proof of the general acceptance of this tenet by the casuists.

Je l'en remerciai, car je n'en avais que trop entendu. Mais pour voir jusqu'où irait une si damnable doctrine, . . .[21]

Pascal is clearly doing his best here to discredit the Jesuits by aligning their doctrine with blatant disregard for secular authority.[22] But when allowances are made for the tactical devices used, the tone of the passages shows his rooted antipathy not merely to the Jesuit principle in question, but also to the aristocratic 'right' and practice it is designed to sanction.

The discussion in the ninth letter of what Christian devotion entails provides further examples of this criticism of Jesuit concessions to contemporary social standards. Pascal's Jesuit is there represented as saying that, since the worldly are commonly frightened off by the excessive rigour of devotion, the members of his order have considered it a step of first importance for the success of their ministry to the privileged classes to remove this obstacle.

. . . pour vous faire voir en détail combien nos Pères en ont ôté de peines, n'est-ce pas une chose bien pleine de consolation pour les ambitieux, d'apprendre qu'ils peuvent conserver une véritable dévotion avec un amour désordonné pour les grandeurs? Eh quoi! mon Père, avec quelque excès qu'ils les recherchent? Oui, dit-il; . . .[23]

---

[19] C. p. 731; G.E. V, p. 92.
[20] C. p. 734; G.E. V, p. 96.
[21] C. p. 734; G.E. V, p. 98.
[22] In the introduction to his English translation of the *Provinciales*, A. J. Krailsheimer notes that "Such deliberate appeals to the civil arm had long been a commonplace of religious controversy, and Pascal knew . . . how easily subversion and heresy could be associated once the seed of doubt was sown." Pascal, *The Provincial Letters*, Harmondsworth 1967, p. 21. Cf. also Bénichou, *op. cit.*, p. 123.
[23] C. pp. 756-7; G.E. V, p. 199. Cf. *ibid.* "Voilà, lui dis-je, de belles décisions en faveur de la vanité, de l'ambition, et de l'avarice." C. p. 758; G.E. V, p. 201. And in the *Pensées* Pascal affirms: "Les conditions les plus aisées à vivre selon le

Once again it is not simply the Jesuit attempt to accommodate the requirements of what he believes is true Christian piety to worldly ambition that Pascal is concerned to censure here. The criticism, veiled though it may be, goes deeper. What he is attacking behind the Jesuits is the way in which the privileged orders in society have come to regard such ambition as normal and even desirable, accepting it as the basis of their code of behaviour.

Similar implications lie behind the charge brought against the casuists' attenuations, in favour of the wealthy, of the established Christian practice of giving alms to relieve the poor. Having cited passages from Cajetan and Aquinas to support the view that Christians are obliged to give all their superfluous wealth in alms, Pascal continues

Et cependant il ne plaît pas à Vasquez qu'on soit obligé d'en donner une partie seulement, tant il a de complaisance pour les riches, de dureté pour les pauvres, et d'opposition à ces sentiments de charité qui font trouver douce la vérité de ces paroles de Saint Grégoire, laquelle paraît si rude aux riches du monde: . . .[24]

Vasquez's consideration for the rich indicates the mainspring, as Pascal would have it, of the Jesuit ethical system, to conform Christian morality to current values. Despite this strategic opposition however, it is plain that Pascal's judgement, at least as it is summarized in the passage quoted from Saint Gregory, involves a reversal of such values. It is because Saint Gregory's opinion – that relieving the hardship of the poor means just restoring to them what is theirs by right – implies the absolute denial of a worldly code grounded in ambition oriented toward self-aggrandizement, that the truth it sets forth appears so hard to the wealthy.

Finally there is a particularly significant passage in the *Second écrit des curés de Paris* where Pascal implies that the aristocratic values which he is concerned to repudiate are the offshoots of man's corrupt nature. One of the reasons given for calling the Jesuits to account is that

Nous les voyons malgré tous les avertissements charitables qu'on leur a donnés . . . autoriser opiniâtrement la vengeance, l'avarice, la volupté, le faux honneur, l'amour-propre et toutes les passions de la nature corrompue, . . .[25]

The Jesuits therefore, in their quest for easier terms of sympathy between God and the nobility, degrade Christian values to conformity with what

monde sont les plus difficiles à vivre selon Dieu; et au contraire: . . . Rien n'est plus aisé que d'être dans une grande charge et dans de grands biens selon le monde; rien n'est plus difficile que d'y vivre selon Dieu, et sans y prendre de part et de goût." L. 693; B. 906.

[24] C. p. 797; G.E. V, p. 372.
[25] C. p. 926; G.E. VII, p. 323.

Pascal regards as the corrupt tendencies of human nature. In this way they undermine what is for him the whole purpose of ethics, to direct men to live up to their own true nature. The evil of casuistry, as practised by the Jesuits for the privileged classes, lies in their attempt to reconcile two fundamentally disparate orders of value. As Pascal sees it they encourage the individual to persist in his pursuit of values belonging to the lower order while guaranteeing him access to those of the higher order without the complete change in manner of life which membership of the higher order involves. They disregard the qualitative difference between the natural and supernatural orders, which in Pascal's view makes it impossible to pass from one to the other without the radical change of direction which only the action of divine grace can produce.

CHAPTER V

PROBLEMS INHERENT IN THE THREE ORDERS
AS APPLIED TO MORAL QUESTIONS

One problem which results from seeing morality in terms of the three orders becomes apparent when Pascal discounts the conscience as a guide to conduct and appeals to the will of God to determine whether acts are right or wrong. The fragment already quoted,[1] where he sets out to justify the stand he takes in the *Provinciales,* shows how the radical disparity between the natural and supernatural orders leads him to this position.

S'ils ne renoncent à la probabilité, leurs bonnes maximes sont aussi peu saintes que les méchantes, car elles sont fondées sur l'autorité humaine. Et ainsi si elles sont plus justes, elles seront plus raisonnables, mais non pas plus saintes; elles tiennent de la tige sauvage sur quoi elles sont entées.[2]

By equating from an ethical point of view good Jesuit maxims with evil ones, simply because both have a common origin in mere human authority, and by setting up *sainteté* as the criterion of judgement, Pascal emphasizes his conception of true moral principles as grounded in revealed precepts. Since moral worth is denied to acts in the natural order the conscience cannot serve as the criterion of true morality, and it will be necessary to look to some authority with supernatural credentials.

But when Pascal, like Nicole,[3] reserves to the authority of Scripture the means of discovering what man should do, refusing him any native

---

[1] Cf. above, p. 11.
[2] L. 916; B. 920.
[3] "L'Ecriture sainte et la doctrine de l'Eglise nous obligent de regarder la volonté de Dieu ... comme la règle de nos devoirs, qui nous prescrit ce que nous devons faire; ... *Essais de morale,* vol. I, 6th ed, Paris 1682, p. 81. "... Dieu qui ne peut dispenser les hommes de vivre selon sa vérité, qui est leur règle immuable et essentielle, a voulu, pour leur faciliter le moyen de la suivre, faire écrire ses loix dans les Ecritures, ... Ainsi consulter Dieu sur ses actions, n'est autre chose que consulter les règles de l'Evangile, pour s'acquitter dans toutes les rencontres particulières de ce que Dieu nous y demande." *Essais,* vol. IV, 4th ed., Paris 1687, p. 379.

power of deciding between right and wrong, he seems to overlook the independent moral judgement which this recommendation involves. By choosing the authority of the Christian tradition for guidance on ethical questions the individual shows that he already knows the difference between right and wrong in general,[4] for otherwise his choice would be quite arbitrary. In other words he performs just such an act of independent moral judgement as Pascal denies him the capacity to make. And as far as Pascal himself is concerned he obviously has no doubt about the superior moral value of the Christian tradition, but does not admit that he has discerned this by his own moral judgement and accepted its authority accordingly. He does not appear to see that while men may need to have the details of right conduct set before them, this does not mean that they cannot recognize its validity when it is presented to them. If man's incapacity is as radical as some of Pascal's statements seem to suggest it is difficult to see what he hoped to achieve by writing the *Provinciales*. The whole purpose of that work is to vindicate what he regards as the true Christian ethic, and discredit what he considers the Jesuits' diluted version of it, by placing the evidence before the individual and leaving it to his moral judgement to decide the case. There is nothing to show that Pascal believes this power of moral judgement must be enlightened by grace in order to see the discrepancy and appreciate his point of view. The immediate popular success of the *Provinciales* tells against such an interpretation. Rather Pascal appeals for his verdict to the individual's native power of deciding between right and wrong; so that to this extent it might be argued that it is at the bar of conscience that Pascal indicts the Jesuits.[5]

The inconsistency in Pascal's approach becomes even more obvious when he shelters behind an appeal to occult justice in order to avoid having to explain how the guilt which has accrued from original sin can be transmitted by 'seminal identity' to all men.[6] Since he rejects the conscience as moral criterion, because good acts belong to an order of values inaccessible to man's natural faculties, it is not surprising to find him denying its validity as a test of the truth of doctrine. In the *Pensées* he urges the need for man to acknowledge the will of God, not only as the principal sanction in morals, but as the standard of what is good and

---

[4] Cf. Hastings Rashdall, *The Theory of Good and Evil*, 2nd ed., Oxford 1924, vol. II, pp. 174-188, 291-4.

[5] Cf. above, p. 26.

[6] For an account of the Augustinian conception on which Pascal's version of the doctrine is clearly based see N.P. Williams, *The Ideas of the Fall and of Original Sin*, London 1927, pp. 372-382.

just and what is bad and unjust.[7] And to emphasize that there is no common measure between man's justice and God's justice he calls on a mathematical analogy.

L'unité jointe à l'infini ne l'augmente de rien, . . . Le fini s'anéantit en présence de l'infini, et devient un pur néant. Ainsi notre esprit devant Dieu, ainsi notre justice devant la justice divine. Il n'y a pas si grande disproportion entre notre justice et celle de Dieu, qu'entre l'unité et l'infini.[8]

Although the disparity between the two sorts of justice is said to be less than that between a unit and the infinite this is small consolation. The force of the comparison is clear when Pascal cites the mystery of the transmission of guilt incurred by Adam's sin to show how man's inability to conceive God's justice disqualifies him from judging what is or is not consistent with it. In this context he derides human justice.

. . . il est sans doute qu'il n'y a rien qui choque plus notre raison que de dire que le péché du premier homme ait rendu coupables ceux qui, étant si éloignés de cette source, semblent incapables d'y participer. Cet écoulement ne nous paraît pas seulement impossible, il nous semble même très injuste; car qu'y a-t-il de plus contraire aux règles de notre misérable justice que de damner éternellement un enfant incapable de volonté, pour un péché où il paraît avoir si peu de part, qu'il est commis six mille ans avant qu'il fût en être? [9]

When Pascal attempts to justify God's action in imputing the guilt of Adam's sin to all men, by affirming that in the things of God reason is out of its depth, one of his own cautionary jottings seems to have slipped his memory.

Si on choque les principes de la raison, notre religion sera absurde et ridicule.[10]

Since he admits that nothing is more shocking to human reason than the doctrine in question, it can be rejected according to his own terms as absurd and ridiculous. Far from being miserable, as Pascal scornfully labels it, human justice turns out to be the proper criterion to which to refer. Moreover, when he maintains that the human idea of justice is no measure of what 'justice' is as applied to God, so that the justice ascribed to God is not simply what men recognize as justice in a greatly intensified degree, but a different quality altogether, he is guilty of intentionally using the same word to signify things he plainly regards as entirely different.[11]

[7] Cf. below, p. 78.
[8] L. 418; B. 233.
[9] L. 131; B. 434.
[10] L. 173; B. 273.
[11] Cf. John Stuart Mill's discussion of Dean H. L. Mansel's position on this question, which closely resembles that of Pascal, in *An Examination of Sir William Hamilton's Philosophy*, 2nd ed., London 1865, pp. 98-102.

There is no indication that Pascal extends the impossibility of knowing divine justice to a belief in the purely negative character of all words applied to God. In the *Prière pour le bon usage des maladies,* for example, he addresses God as

Seigneur, dont l'esprit est si bon et si doux en toutes choses ... faites-moi la grâce de n'agir pas en païen dans l'état où votre justice m'a réduit.... [12]

Yet on what grounds, especially in such a context, can Pascal ascribe to God the normal human qualities of goodness and gentleness when he holds so emphatically that the justice which marks God's dealings with men is utterly unlike all human conceptions of it?

Pascal's attitude to the Calvinist doctrine of grace and predestination, as he describes it in the *Premier écrit sur la grâce,* is particularly interesting here. The summary which he proposes includes the tenets of absolute predestination, divine causation of Adam's sin, the restriction of Christ's redemptive grace to those originally marked out for salvation and the irrevocable deprivation of the remainder. It is immaterial for the present purpose whether or not this is an accurate account of the Calvinist position, since it is Pascal's comments upon it that are significant.

Voilà l'opinion épouvantable de ces hérétiques, injurieuse à Dieu et insupportable aux hommes. Voilà les blasphèmes par lesquels ils établissent en Dieu une volonté absolue et sans aucune prévision de mérite ou de péché pour damner ou pour sauver ses créatures. ... cette opinion abominable ... [elle] blesse le sens commun ... [elle] est si horrible, et frappe d'abord l'esprit avec tant de force par la vue de la cruauté de Dieu envers ses créatures, qu'elle est insupportable.[13]

Now it is quite clear that Pascal rejects this doctrine because it contains elements which affront his moral consciousness, his own idea of justice and what he conceives by analogy to be the nature of divine justice. But despite this he refuses to allow equally justified objections to the doctrine of arbitrary selection of the elect from the 'massa damnata', although it is every bit as 'injurious to God' and 'insupportable to men' as the Calvinist one.

In the *Pensées* he condemns precisely the sort of anthropomorphism on which he himself relies in this denunciation of the Calvinist doctrine.

"Les hommes, n'ayant pas accoutumé de former le mérite, mais seulement le récompenser où ils le trouvent formé, jugent de Dieu par eux-mêmes." [14]

[12] C. p. 605; G.E. IX, p. 323.
[13] C. pp. 951-2, 956; G.E. XI, pp. 133-4, 139.
[14] L. 935; B. 490.

Thus when men project on to God their notion of justice, which consists essentially in a system of penalties and rewards assigned to appropriate acts, they entirely fail to recognize that it is God himself who inspires or motivates any good action worthy of reward that man may perform. This means that divine justice has a creative dimension totally lacking in human justice, which sets it outside the range of human experience.

And in another fragment Pascal denies completely man's competence to judge what is in harmony with God's moral character.

Mon Dieu! que ce sont de sots discours! Dieu aurait-il fait le monde pour le damner? demanderait-il tant, de gens si faibles? etc. Pyrrhonisme est le remède à ce mal, et rabattra cette vanité.[15]

Man cannot reason therefore about what God must be like or what he must do, nor can he reject revealed doctrines as incompatible with God's nature, since it is only through revelation that he has any knowledge of the divine attributes. The scheme of divine providence is beyond the reach of man's natural capacities, so that instead of presuming to determine what is consistent with it he must be content simply to believe without questioning what is disclosed to him in revelation.

It is clear from Pascal's definition of theology in the *Préface pour le traité du vide* that the doctrine of the three orders, by establishing a difference in kind between the natural and supernatural orders, leads him to remove the whole content of revelation from the scope of moral criticism. Since revealed authority is the appropriate source of information for theology

... pour donner la certitude entière des matières les plus incompréhensibles à la raison, il suffit de les faire voir dans les livres sacrés ... parce que ses principes sont au-dessus de la nature et de la raison, et que, l'esprit de l'homme étant trop faible pour y arriver pas ses propres efforts, il ne peut parvenir à ces hautes intelligences s'il n'y est porté par une force toute-puissante et surnaturelle.[16]

---

[15] L. 896; B. 390. Pascal's English contemporary John Selden uses a telling example to emphasize his similar view of the disproportion between human and divine attributes. "Nay wee measure the excellency of God from ourselves, wee measure his goodness his Justice, his wisdome by something wee call just good or wise in our selves, and in soe doeing wee judge proporconably to the Country fellow in the play, who said, If hee were a King hee would live like a Lord, and have pease and Bacon every day and a Whipp that cry'de Slash." *Table Talk of John Selden*, ed. Sir Frederick Pollock, London 1927, p. 77.

[16] C. p. 530; G.E. II, p. 131. Thus in the *Troisième écrit sur la grâce*, in his exposition of the Augustinian doctrine of predestination, Pascal cites the authority of Saint Augustine for the view that it is "par un jugement caché" that God determines to abandon the damned to their own free will, and adds "Enfin ce n'est pour aucune raison qui puisse nous être connue, puisque c'est par un jugement occulte; ce qui est d'une si grande force, que je vous la laisse à exagérer." C. pp. 991-2; G.E. XI, pp. 204-5. Cf. C. p. 1044; G.E. XI, p. 295.

Revelation therefore is self-certifying, it carries its own guarantee of veracity, so that belief in it does not depend on the morality of its contents. But to argue, as Pascal does here, that man's faculties are too weak for him to understand the content of revelation without supernatural aid, does not resolve the problem of how the authenticity of an alleged revelation is to be decided if he cannot trust his own moral consciousness for that purpose.

Despite his attempt to justify the difficulties of revelation by scepticism about man's natural powers, it is the ordinary human notion of recompense which is uppermost in Pascal's mind when he speaks of God's 'justice' toward the reprobate, contrasting it with the mercy he shows to his elect. In this context the word obviously carries the meaning of punishment.

Il faut que la justice de Dieu soit énorme comme sa miséricorde. Or, la justice envers les réprouvés est moins énorme et doit moins choquer que la miséricorde envers les élus.[17]

And the most frequent use of the term in the *Ecrits sur la grâce* is in the same sense of retributive justice.

Dans l'état d'innocence, Dieu ne pouvait avec justice damner aucun des hommes, ...Dans l'état de corruption, Dieu pouvait avec justice damner la masse entière; ...[18]

Pour sauver ses élus, Dieu a envoyé Jésus-Christ pour satisfaire à sa justice, et pour mériter de sa miséricorde la grâce de Rédemption, ...[19]

It would be difficult to provide a more apt illustration of the system of sanctions, which for Pascal represents the application of human justice, than the procedure outlined in the last extract. A sin has been committed; someone must atone, and, by submitting to the punishment, induce the judge to forego the sentence of those who have won his favour. The fact that it is Christ who atones, and that God is responsible for his substitution, in no way alters the conclusion that on this principle the cornerstone of divine justice is the necessity of requital.

Furthermore, on those occasions in the *Provinciales* where Pascal mentions divine justice it is almost invariably to point out that it is not essentially different from human justice; that those crimes which infringe civil law, and are offensive to man's sense of justice of which laws are the concrete embodiment, are immeasurably more abhorrent in the eyes of God; that divine justice is undoubtedly superior to human justice, but

[17] L. 418; B. 233.
[18] C. p. 952; G.E. XI, p. 135.
[19] C. p. 966; G.E. XI, p. 149.

that there exists no fundamental contradiction between them. Indeed some of the most telling criticism of what he considers to be the immoral consequences of Jesuit casuistry rests upon precisely that assumption. This is plain when Pascal objects to the practice of permitting an act in theory, even though it may be contrary to the commandments of God, while prohibiting its actual performance out of respect for the civil authorities.

Je ne vous reproche pas de craindre les juges, mais de ne craindre que les juges. C'est cela que je blâme; parce que c'est faire Dieu moins ennemi des crimes que les hommes. . . . quand vous prétendez que ce qui est trop criminel pour être souffert par les hommes, soit innocent et juste aux yeux de Dieu qui est la justice même, que faites-vous autre chose, sinon montrer à tout le monde que, . . . vous êtes hardis contre Dieu, et timide envers les hommes? [20]

Pascal is in effect arguing here that what offends man's sense of justice must affect God in the same way but in a greatly intensified degree, because, as justice itself, he is the ultimate source of man's idea of justice. This kind of argument comes very close to constituting an inference drawn from the nature of man to the nature of God. Yet in view of his categorical assertions that there is no common measure between human justice and divine justice, and that the latter may differ as far from the former as God himself differs from man, Pascal, to be consistent, would have to concede the possibility that what men refuse to permit as too criminal is innocent and just in the sight of God. Since man does not know what justice is as it exists in God, it is clearly just as impossible for him to say what it is not as to say what it is. Pascal's agnosticism here, whether he likes it or not, is a two-edged weapon that cuts both ways.

In the fourteenth letter he maintains, in accordance with Pauline teaching, that God has bestowed on temporal princes the right to administer the power of life and death over their subjects, but that

. . . comme c'est Dieu qui leur a donné ce droit, il les oblige à l'exercer ainsi qu'il le ferait lui-même, c'est-à-dire avec justice, . . . [21]

As God is justice and wisdom itself, in the course of exercising this right they must, to avoid committing murder, act both by God's authority and in accordance with his justice. But if men, whatever their office, are to act in accordance with the canons of divine justice this means they must be able to, so that there can be no reason for them not to understand how it works.

[20] C. p. 815; G.E. VI, pp. 37-8.
[21] C. p. 820; G.E. VI, p. 133.

At the end of the same letter Pascal censures the Jesuits for authorizing the outlawed practice of duelling.

Mais on doit louer Dieu de ce qu'il a éclairé l'esprit du roi par des lumières plus pures que celles de votre théologie. Ses édits si sévères sur ce sujet ... Il a arrêté par la crainte de la rigueur de sa justice ceux qui n'étaient pas arrêtés par la crainte de la justice de Dieu; ...[22]

Here again the context makes it plain that God's justice differs from the king's justice only as greater in degree, with the characteristic element of both, as Pascal describes them, consisting in the threat of punishment to the transgressor.

It is clear from Pascal's linguistic usage then that when he distinguishes between what he claims are two different sorts of justice he is using the term 'justice' in an equivocal way, since it does not undergo a regular change in meaning when he transfers it from the human to the divine sphere. Although he denies the possibility of any common measure between the two, on those occasions when divine justice is actually in question he speaks of it in terms which show quite unmistakably that it operates in exactly the same fashion as human justice, on the principle that merit should be rewarded and shortcomings punished. In fact one of the criticisms levelled at the Calvinist doctrine of predestination is that it represents God as failing to take account in his election of 'merit' and 'sin'; in other words as acting otherwise than by the principle that merit should be rewarded and shortcomings punished. This, together with the fact that according to the *Provinciales* divine justice is administered and dispensed by human agents who do not necessarily belong to the order of charity, points to the conclusion that Pascal is not entirely consistent in applying the notion of the three orders to ethical questions.

[22] C. p. 831; G.E. VI, p. 155.

CHAPTER VI

PASCAL'S TELEOLOGICAL APPROACH TO ETHICS IN THE *PENSÉES*

The tendency to depreciate natural virtue, latent in the doctrine of the three orders, is strengthened by the teleological approach to moral questions which Pascal favours in the *Pensées*. The good acts which it is man's duty to perform are beyond his natural powers because his end, relation to which determines the moral quality of human acts, is supernatural. Man cannot reach this end by natural means, yet no act which does not help him to attain it can be called good.

It is, however, by examining human nature, and by observing human life in this world, that Pascal believes the individual becomes aware that his true destiny lies beyond the natural order. In this context he emphasizes particularly man's desire for truth and happiness.[1] The stock proof that something has gone wrong with human nature, which depends upon establishing its dichotomy and manifest incompleteness, brings this out. The form of argument is familiar enough. Although man is impelled by his very nature to embark on the quest for truth and happiness, so that his native capacity for it seems unimpaired, the quest inevitably ends in disillusionment. The desire for happiness, which is part of man's nature and underlies all his other desires, remains unsatisfied. And in this universal consciousness, as he declares it to be, of the hiatus in man's nature Pascal finds evidence of an historic fall from a state where that nature was complete.

---

[1] Pascal does not define what he understands by 'truth' in this context. But in view of the constant association of the two terms 'truth' and 'happiness', in the fragments from the *Pensées*, it is clear that he follows Saint Augustine in believing that the attainment of final happiness consists in vision of the truth. And, since truth is identified with God, only in some form of beatific vision will the desire for full and perfect truth be satisfied. Cf. L. 99; B. 536. L. 926; B. 582. L. 974; B. 949. For Saint Augustine's views on this question see E. Gilson, *Introduction à l'étude de Saint Augustin*, pp. 1-10, and J. Burnaby, *Amor Dei: A Study of the Religion of Saint Augustine*, London 1938, pp. 153-8.

Nous souhaitons la vérité, et ne trouvons en nous qu'incertitude. Nous recherchons le bonheur, et ne trouvons que misère et mort. Nous sommes incapables de ne pas souhaiter la vérité et le bonheur, et sommes incapables ni de certitude ni de bonheur.[2]
... c'est être malheureux que de vouloir et ne pouvoir. Or [l'homme] veut être heureux, et assuré de quelque vérité; et cependant il ne peut ni savoir, ni ne désirer point de savoir.[3]
Voilà l'état où les hommes sont aujourd'hui. Il leur reste quelque instinct impuissant du bonheur de leur première nature, et ils sont plongés dans les misères de leur aveuglement et de leur concupiscence, ...[4]
Instinct, raison. – Nous avons une impuissance de prouver, invincible à tout le dogmatisme. Nous avons une idée de la vérité, invincible à tout le pyrrhonisme.[5]
Tous les hommes recherchent d'être heureux: cela est sans exception; quelques différents moyens qu'ils y emploient, ils tendent tous à ce but.[6]
Notre instinct nous fait sentir qu'il faut chercher notre bonheur hors de nous.[7]
Nonobstant ces misères, il veut être heureux, et ne veut être qu'heureux, et ne peut ne vouloir pas l'être; ...[8]
... enfin si l'homme n'avait jamais été corrompu, il jouirait dans son innocence et de la vérité et de la félicité avec assurance; et si l'homme n'avait jamais été que corrompu, il n'aurait aucune idée ni de la vérité ni de la béatitude. Mais, malheureux que nous sommes, et plus que s'il n'y avait point de grandeur dans notre condition, nous avons une idée du bonheur et ne pouvons y arriver; nous sentons une image de la vérité, et ne possédons que le mensonge: ...[9]

The presence of these seemingly incompatible elements in man's nature, as it now is, proves, according to Pascal, that "nous avons été dans un degré de perfection dont nous sommes malheureusement déchus." [10] The argument testifies to the importance he ascribes to the search for truth and happiness in the moral life of man. For the present dim, but unmistakable, awareness of truth and happiness, which persists despite all vicissitudes and prevents man finding any real or lasting satisfaction in the objects that surround him in his actual condition, represents the empty trace of his former "grandeur". The desire for truth and happiness is, therefore, simply the expression of man's desire to regain what Pascal holds is his true nature.

It is this, seen in the perspective of the Fall, that enables him to go further and identify the object that will satisfy man's desire for happiness with the end for which he has been created. The fragment from the

---

[2] L. 401; B. 437.
[3] L. 75; B. 389.
[4] L. 149; B. 430.
[5] L. 406; B. 395.
[6] L. 148; B. 425.
[7] L. 143; B. 464.
[8] L. 134; B. 169.
[9] L. 131; B. 434.
[10] *Ibid.*

Pensées where he contrasts the two points of view from which he alleges it is possible to judge human nature shows how he considers the question of man's end in terms of the familiar "grandeur-misère" opposition, and also how he sets up this end as the criterion of action.

La nature de l'homme se considère en deux manières: l'une selon sa fin, et alors il est grand et incomparable: l'autre selon la multitude, comme on juge de la nature du cheval et du chien, par la multitude, d'y voir la course, 'et animum arcendi'; et alors l'homme est abject et vil. Et voilà les deux voies qui en font juger diversement, . . .[11]

Man's nature when regarded in the light of the end, to which Pascal believes his potential and aspirations point, is judged therefore "grand et incomparable"; a judgement which reflects back on the worth of the pursuit of truth and happiness. M. Brunschvicg's interpretation of this contrast between "multitude" and "fin", to mean the opposition of the generality of cases, which defines man's real nature, to the ideal nature, which is his true destiny,[12] seems to me misleading. Quite apart from the fact that the whole drift of the *Pensées* is to show that what is here called "la multitude" does not correspond to man's real nature, the term "fin" is not used in Pascal's vocabulary to mean nature, construed even in an ideal sense. Man's end, wherein he will find fulfilment, is always defined as something outside and beyond himself. Nor can his true destiny be to attain an ideal nature, since that destiny is an otherworldly one which is achieved only by reaching the vision of God. That is why Pascal is concerned to underline those aspirations native to man which point beyond him to the infinite and eternal, as the end which alone will satisfy the needs of his nature. Man's nature, then, with its unrealized capacity for truth and happiness, bears witness to its otherworldly destiny.

There is, nevertheless, a curious inconsistency in Pascal's reasoning in this passage. The adjectives, "abject et vil", which he maintains are appropriate to describe man's nature assessed according to his actual performance in the course of life, "selon la multitude", are obviously pejorative. The estimate cannot, therefore, have been made "selon la multitude", from a purely external point of view, as it might be of a horse or dog. In that case the standard of judgement is the actual performance of a normal horse or dog. The assessment is based on what the object is, not on what it ought to be. Since Pascal plainly uses the noun "l'homme" to denote mankind at large, he must, in order to judge humanity "abject et vil", appeal beyond what men's performance shows

---

[11] L. 127; B. 415.
[12] Blaise Pascal, *Pensées et opuscules,* ed. L. Brunschvicg, p. 514, n.l.

their nature to be to some further criterion. Even when he professes to judge man's nature "selon la multitude" Pascal, then, is in fact measuring his achievements against the end for which his aspirations show he is destined.

The desire for truth and happiness is not to be regarded merely as the pointer to man's final end; it also represents the pursuit of his true good. In a long fragment from the *Pensées* Pascal declares that all men without exception seek happiness in an indeterminate sense, and that this desire forms the dominant motive which actuates all human behaviour.

Et cependant, depuis un si grand nombre d'années, jamais personne, sans la foi, n'est arrivé à ce point où tous visent continuellement. . . . Une épreuve si longue, si continuelle et si uniforme, devrait bien nous convaincre de notre impuissance d'arriver au bien par nos efforts; . . .[13]

All men desire to be happy therefore, but there is no universal desire for happiness in what Thomas Aquinas calls its "specific notion",[14] no agreement about the object outside the self in which happiness is to be found. The fragment concludes with an account of the great variety of opinions held about where the true good is to be sought. Pascal argues that on this question those who have come closest to the truth hold that it cannot consist in particular things, in which one man's gain is another's loss, but that it must be such that all men may possess it at once without anyone being worse off because someone else has it. Man's true good must be the universal good, which at once transcends and includes the good of every individual.

Ils ont compris que le vrai bien devrait être tel . . . et leur raison est que ce désir étant naturel à l'homme, puisqu'il est nécessairement dans tous, et qu'il ne peut pas ne le pas avoir, . . .[15]

The desire for truth and happiness and the pursuit of the true good are therefore the same thing. And Pascal's insistence that all men's efforts to accomplish it by themselves have left this fundamental need of their nature unsupplied shows that he intends by the expression "le vrai bien" something apart from man's own peculiar goodness, in the sense of a native potential which merely wants to be developed.

According to Pascal the universal good is to be found, not in any creature or created object, but in God alone. In the same fragment he argues that, since the basic desire for happiness remains unsatisfied by the outcome of all the particular choices it dictates,

---

[13] L. 148; B. 425.
[14] *Summa Theologica,* Ia IIae, Q. 5, a. 8.
[15] L. 148; B. 425.

...ce gouffre infini ne peut être rempli que par un objet infini et immuable, c'est-à-dire que par Dieu même.

Lui seul est son véritable bien; et depuis qu'il l'a quitté, c'est une chose étrange, qu'il n'y a rien dans la nature qui n'ait été capable de lui en tenir la place:...[16]

God alone therefore is capable of supplying the need of man's nature. In scholastic terms he is the good connatural to man, and accordingly the goal, "fin",[17] to which he is destined. Pascal makes the same point in the *Entretien avec M. de Saci,* where the possibility of attaining the supreme good is said to depend upon the existence of God. Epictetus and Montaigne are described as the most illustrious exponents of the two most famous philosophical sects which are alone

...conformes à la raison, puisqu'on ne peut suivre qu'une de ces deux routes, savoir: ou qu'il y a un Dieu, et lors il y place son souverain bien; ou qu'il est incertain, et qu'alors le vrai bien l'est aussi, puisqu'il en est incapable.[18]

Further examples of this alignment occur as follows in the *Pensées:*

Que les biens temporels sont faux, et que le vrai bien est d'être uni à Dieu. Ps. 143.[19]
...ces oppositions que nous avons à Dieu et à notre propre bien.[20]
Le bonheur n'est ni hors de nous, ni dans nous; il est en Dieu, et hors et dans nous.[21]
Si l'homme n'est fait pour Dieu, pourquoi n'est-il heureux qu'en Dieu?[22]
Seconde partie: Félicité de l'homme avec Dieu.[23]
Le Dieu des Chrétiens est un Dieu qui fait sentir à l'âme qu'il est son unique bien, que tout son repos est en lui,...[24]

In the short treatise *Sur la conversion du pécheur* the soul recognizes that it is a condition of attaining to full and permanent happiness

...de se joindre à un bien véritable et subsistant par lui-même, qui pût la soutenir et durant et après cette vie.[25]

The culmination of the search for this true good is reached when the soul is brought to see that God is the sovereign good for which it thirsts,

---

[16] *Ibid.*
[17] Cf. from an early letter to Mme Périer: "...il n'y a que Dieu qui doive être la dernière fin comme lui seul est le vrai principe." C. pp. 484-5; G.E. II, p. 250. In the brief *Sur la conversion du pécheur,* the soul in its aspiration after God is represented as desiring that he should be "lui-même son chemin, son objet et sa dernière fin." C. p. 551; G.E.X., p. 426.
[18] C. p. 571; G.E. IV, p. 51.
[19] L. 453; B. 610.
[20] L. 149; B. 430.
[21] L. 407; B. 465.
[22] L. 399; B. 438.
[23] L. 6; B. 60.
[24] L. 460; B. 544.
[25] C. p. 549; G.E. X, p. 423.

and that there is nothing more lovable than him. Similarly in the fifth strophe of the *Prière pour le bon usage des maladies* Pascal writes

O mon Dieu, qu'un cœur est heureux qui peut aimer un objet si charmant, ... O mon Dieu, qu'une âme est heureuse dont vous êtes les délices, ... Que son bonheur est ferme et durable, ...[26]

In the eighteenth *Provinciale* also God is identified with the good and man's ultimate happiness.

... Dieu change le cœur de l'homme par une douceur céleste qu'il y répand, qui ... fait que l'homme ... conçoit du dégoût pour les délices du péché qui le séparent du bien incorruptible; trouvant sa plus grande joie dans le Dieu qui le charme, il s'y porte infailliblement de lui-même; ...[27]

Man's desire for happiness is fully realized therefore, according to Pascal, only when his whole life is ordered to God, his end and supreme good.

Descartes's approach to this question of the good provides an interesting contrast with Pascal's. In an important letter to Queen Christina of Sweden, in November 1647, Descartes draws attention to the distinction between the supreme good considered objectively, which can only be defined as God, since he is incomparably more perfect than any creature; and the supreme good considered subjectively, in relation to human nature

... et en ce sens, je ne vois rien que nous devions estimer bien, sinon ce qui nous appartient en quelque façon, et qui est tel, que c'est perfection pour nous de l'avoir.[28]

Now Pascal in effect telescopes these alternative points of view. He declares that man is unable to find what will appease his natural desire for happiness in any particular good, whether outside himself or in himself. Since the sovereign good considered objectively, God, is alone capable of giving him complete and eternal happiness, it must also constitute the individual's particular good. Descartes, on the other hand, like the ancient philosophers who were not "éclairés de la lumière de la foi",[29] sets out to determine what makes up man's supreme good from the point of view of human nature. This he takes to consist in "... une ferme volonté de bien faire, et au contentement qu'elle produit",[30] and gives as his reason that he knows of no other good either so great or so completely within the range of man's capacity.

[26] C. p. 608; G.E. IX, pp. 328-9.
[27] C. p. 887; G.E. VII, p. 29.
[28] *Œuvres et lettres,* ed. Bridoux, pp. 1281-2.
[29] *Ibid.,* p. 1282.
[30] *Ibid.*

In an earlier letter to Princess Elisabeth of Bohemia, in August 1645, Descartes distinguishes between the sovereign good and the contentment it produces, which he calls beatitude. This beatitude, which is "le motif, ou la fin à laquelle tendent nos actions",[31] he goes on to define as contentment of mind, which amounts to the same thing as a general feeling of satisfaction, and adds that

> ... pour avoir un contentement qui soit solide, il est besoin de suivre la vertu, c'est-à-dire d'avoir une volonté ferme et constante d'exécuter tout ce que nous jugerons être le meilleur, et d'employer toute la force de notre entendement à en bien juger.[32]

Since beatitude has already been described as the contentment of mind which results from possession of the supreme good, it follows that the supreme good is equivalent to virtue as Descartes has defined it. And the reason why the supreme good is identified with virtue is that virtue, alone of the various goods which man may possess, depends entirely on the exercise of his own free will. In Descartes's neo-stoic terms it is no more than appropriate that the supreme good should be achieved by the right exercise of free will, since it is the characteristic distinction of human nature. An extract from another letter to Princess Elisabeth, in the same month, shows just how far Descartes is from agreeing with Pascal in placing the end, wherein the aspirations of man's nature can find fulfilment, in a supernatural good beyond the range of man's natural capacity.

> ... la béatitude consiste, ce me semble, en un parfait contentement d'esprit et une satisfaction intérieure, ... il me semble qu'un chacun se peut rendre content de soi-même et sans rien attendre d'ailleurs, pourvu seulement qu'il observe trois choses, auxquelles se rapportent les trois règles de morale, que j'ai mises dans le *Discours de la Méthode*.[33]

Complying with these three points, outlined in the provisional ethic of the *Discours,* amounts simply to what Descartes defines as following virtue.

Although Pascal maintains that the good as he has defined it is proportionate to man's nature, in the sense that the desire for it is natural to him, he is emphatic that it exceeds man's natural powers.[34] That

---

[31] *Ibid.,* p. 1199.
[32] *Ibid.,* p. 1200.
[33] *Ibid.,* p. 1193.
[34] "Une épreuve si longue, si continuelle et si uniforme, devrait bien nous convaincre de notre impuissance d'arriver au bien par nos efforts; ... Qu'est-ce donc que nous crie cette avidité et cette impuissance, sinon qu'il y a eu autrefois dans l'homme un véritable bonheur, dont il ne lui reste maintenant que la marque et la trace toute vide, et qu'il essaye inutilement de remplir de tout ce qui l'environne, ..." L. 148; B. 425.

much is plain from his repeated assertions of the failure of secular philosophers to find out by themselves what is the supreme good for man, and from the unenviable position to which he assigns the pre-Christian era. The *Pensées* contain numerous references to fruitless attempts by secular thinkers to discover what constitutes the final end of man and his sovereign good.

Recherche du vrai bien. – Le commun des hommes met le bien dans la fortune et dans les biens du dehors, ou au moins dans le divertissement. Les philosophes ont montré la vanité de tout cela et l'ont mis où ils ont pu.[35]
Que l'homme sans la foi ne peut connaître le vrai bien,...[36]
280 sortes de souverains biens dans Montaigne.[37]
Le souverain bien. Dispute du souverain bien.... Il y a contradiction, car ils conseillent enfin de se tuer.[38]
"C'est en vain, ô hommes, que vous cherchez dans vous-mêmes le remède à vos misères. Toutes vos lumières ne peuvent arriver qu'à connaître que ce n'est point dans vous-mêmes que vous trouvez ni la vérité ni le bien. Les philosophes vous l'ont promis, et ils n'ont pu le faire. Ils ne savent ni quel est votre véritable bien,..."[39]

In Pascal's view outside help is needed not merely for man to progress toward the goal of his desires, but even for him to know what the goal is and how he is to achieve it.

Le pyrrhonisme est le vrai. Car, après tout, les hommes avant Jésus-Christ, ne savaient où ils en étaient, ni s'ils étaient grands ou petits. Et ceux qui ont dit l'un ou l'autre n'en savaient rien, et devinaient sans raison et par hasard; et même ils erraient toujours, en excluant l'un ou l'autre. 'Quod ergo ignorantes quaeritis, religio annuntiat vobis.[40]

In other words in the pre-Christian era of history man was debarred from any real knowledge about his nature and end because the Christian revelation had not then occurred: an outlook which coincides with Pascal's uncompromising attitude toward the 'virtuous pagans'.[41] Moreover when he quotes, apparently from memory, the line from *Acts,* 17, 23, where Paul announces to the Areopagites that he has come to declare to them the true God whom they already worship in the guise of the "Unknown God", Pascal, as M. Brunschvicg has noted,[42] changes significantly the meaning of the original. Paul believed that the pagans had glimpsed the

[35] L. 626; B. 462.
[36] L. 148; B. 425.
[37] L. 408; B. 74.
[38] L. 147; B. 361.
[39] L. 149; B. 430.
[40] L. 691; B. 432.
[41] Cf. L. 359; B. 481, and above p. 24.
[42] Blaise Pascal, *Pensées et opuscules*, p. 528, n.1.

truth, whereas, according to Pascal, they have never emerged from error.

The identification of man's pursuit of truth and happiness with that of his true good, and of the attainment of them with the attainment by man of his end, has important implications for Pascal's conception of the dignity that attaches to human thought. He believes this dignity consists in the way man's power of reflexion enables him to act deliberately in view of what he recognizes will lead him toward his end and final happiness. By this means he has access to a higher order than that to which animals belong whose behaviour is purely instinctive.[43]

Pascal follows the scholastic tradition in considering this capacity for thought as the "differentia" that marks man off from inanimate things and the sentient brutes.

Je puis bien concevoir un homme sans mains, pieds, tête, ... Mais je ne puis concevoir l'homme sans pensée: ce serait une pierre ou une brute.[44]

For Pascal it follows not only that, looked at simply as one object among others in nature, man's whole dignity resides in this capacity, but further that ethics can be defined as the right exercise of it.

Toute notre dignité consiste donc en la pensée. C'est de là qu'il faut nous relever ... Travaillons donc à bien penser: voilà le principe de la morale.[45]

The same view is reiterated in another significant fragment, where Pascal goes on to outline the framework within which this right thinking should be conducted.

L'homme est visiblement fait pour penser; c'est toute sa dignité et tout son mérite, et tout son devoir est de penser comme il faut. Or l'ordre de la pensée est de commencer par soi, et par son auteur et sa fin.[46]

Despite the subjective emphasis here, Pascal's recommendation cannot be taken to mean that he regards the end as something human. In his terms it would be circular to define the end as man's dignity as a rational animal, or anything of that sort.

When these statements are set alongside the definition of man's end, as what will satisfy the desire for truth and happiness inalienable from his nature, it becomes plain to what extent Pascal's ethic is preoccupied with the individual's needs and their satisfaction. Such a frankly eudae-monistic moral outlook, characteristic of his age,[47] results in a con-

---

[43] Cf. *Préface pour le traité du vide,* C. p. 533; G.E. II, p. 138.
[44] L. 111; B. 339.
[45] L. 200; B. 347.
[46] L. 620; B. 146.
[47] Even in the eighteenth century in France this kind of moral outlook was predominant according to Gustave Lanson: "Si l'on excepte la morale de Rousseau,

ception of ethics as primarily concerned, not with abstract notions of justice or duty, nor even with practical "bienfaisance", but with problems relating to the individual's hopes and fears about his condition and destiny. For Pascal, as for Saint Augustine,[48] the vital question is: what is the ultimate good in which happiness is to be found? And not until the satisfactory answer to this question has been given does he consider it possible to go on and ask the further question: what course of action will be appropriate for a particular individual in a given instance? On this view the principle of right action is the desire for the supreme good that is man's end, wherein his yearning for happiness will be supplied, not the desire simply to do what one ought. As will appear, Pascal regards acts done for duty's sake as those which are properly ordered to man's ultimate goal.

Two further passages from the *Pensées* show how he considers the dignity of human thought wholly dependent on its being used to direct man to the goal of his existence. In the second half of the fragment already quoted, where he insists on the rightful priority in the "ordre de pensée" of man's own nature, ground and end, he goes on to enumerate what supersedes these in the thinking of the mass of men.

Or à quoi pense le monde? Jamais à cela; mais à danser, à jouer du luth, à chanter, à faire des vers, à courir la bague, etc., à se battre, à se faire roi, sans penser à ce que c'est qu'être roi, et qu'être homme.[49]

The picture presented by this misuse, as it appears to him, of the precious capacity which alone sets man at an advantage over the physical order by enabling him to reflect on the ends of his actions – allowing it to become absorbed in such aimless and frivolous pursuits – draws from Pascal the following conclusion:

Pensée: – Toute la dignité de l'homme est en la pensée. Mais qu'est-ce que cette pensée? Qu'elle est sotte!
La pensée est donc une chose admirable et incomparable par sa nature. Il

---

... toutes les morales se ramènent à la morale du bonheur, à celle de l'intérêt bien entendu, et à celle de la bienfaisance." *La transformation des idées morales et la naissance des morales rationnelles de 1680 à 1715,* pp. 7-8. The originality of Rousseau's approach to ethics is emphasized by Ernst Cassirer also in *The Philosophy of the Enlightenment,* Boston 1955, pp. 153 ff.
[48] Etienne Gilson maintains that it is "un fait capital pour l'intelligence de l'augustinisme, que la sagesse, objet de la philosophie, se soit toujours confondue pour [Augustin] avec la béatitude. Ce qu'il cherche, c'est un bien tel que sa possession comble tout désir ... Cet eudémonisme foncier ... ce qui l'inquiète surtout, c'est le problème de sa destinée"; ... *Introduction à l'étude de Saint Augustin,* p. 1. Cf. pp. 7 ff. The same point is made by E. Portalié, *Saint Augustin,* in *Dictionnaire de Théologie Catholique,* t, I. Paris 1902, col. 2432-3.
[49] L. 620; B. 146.

fallait qu'elle eût d'étranges défauts pour être méprisable; mais elle en a de tels que rien n'est plus ridicule. Qu'elle est grande par sa nature! qu'elle est basse par ses défauts! [50]

In bringing out the contrast between the promise and the condition of this natural capacity Pascal overlooks perhaps the distinction between the power of thought and the actual content of thought. It seems likely that the defects to which he refers here relate more to content, to the way thought is ordered so that it tends to become engrossed in what he regards as futile distractions. But in any event Pascal is clearly convinced that the power of thought retains its dignity only so long as it is occupied with objects which will help man to achieve his supreme good and final happiness.

Pascal attributes man's failure to observe the proper order of thought, and so to pursue the right end in conduct, to the influence of the passions. By clouding his mind they make it difficult for man to see clearly the good he should seek.

Contrariétés. ... Que l'homme maintenant s'estime son prix ... il a en lui la capacité de connaître la vérité et d'être heureux; mais il n'a point de vérité, ou constante, ou satisfaisante.

Je voudrais donc porter l'homme à désirer d'en trouver, à être prêt, et dégagé des passions, pour la suivre où il la trouvera, sachant combien sa connaissance s'est obscurcie par les passions; je voudrais bien qu'il haït en soi la concupiscence qui le détermine d'elle-même, afin qu'elle ne l'aveuglât point pour faire son choix, et qu'elle ne l'arrêtât point quand il aura choisi.[51]

The aim of the programme of moral direction outlined here is to promote the pursuit of truth and happiness. And a short passage from the *De l'art de persuader,* where he describes how the will is activated, sets out the reason why it is necessary to take such steps to ensure that men will not allow deceptive influences in the form of the passions to sway them in this matter.

... [les] principes et les premiers moteurs [des actions] de la volonté sont de certains désirs naturels et communs à tous les hommes, comme le désir d'être heureux, que personne ne peut pas ne pas avoir, outre plusieurs objets particuliers que chacun suit pour y arriver, et qui, ayant la force de nous plaire, sont aussi forts, quoique pernicieux en effet, pour faire agir la volonté, que s'ils faisaient son véritable bonheur.[52]

The will, then, is the faculty by which man is drawn to desire conclusive happiness. Since this desire is part of his nature it is inescapable. But different means, which will not in fact serve its purpose, may be adopted

[50] L. 756; B. 365.
[51] L. 119; B. 423. Cf. *Quatrième écrit sur la grâce,* C. p. 1033; G.E. XI, p. 258.
[52] C. p. 593; G.E. IX, p. 273.

to satisfy this desire. Part of a fragment from the *Pensées,* already referred to, amplifies the basic notion here.

Tous les hommes recherchent d'être heureux: ... quelques différents moyens qu'ils y emploient, ils tendent tous à ce but. ... La volonté [ne] fait jamais la moindre démarche que vers cet objet. C'est le motif de toutes les actions de tous les hommes, ...[53]

Clearly Pascal's concern to promote the desire for happiness, which he declares is natural to all men and forms the most powerful motive of human behaviour, does not involve sanctioning whatever can give pleasure to man. For some things which can do this, and seem to be steps toward happiness, will actually turn man away from it. And because the will is apt to be misled by these false steps from the proper path to true happiness, Pascal insists that man's whole attention should be focussed on the goal of his desires.[54]

There is again an interesting contrast with Pascal's view here in Descartes's basically scholastic conception of the relation between the passions and the will. In his *Traité des passions de l'âme* Descartes maintains that the will, although powerless to subdue violent passions, is not necessarily carried away by them itself, and moreover has the means to thwart even such passions as these.

Le plus que la volonté puisse faire pendant que cette émotion est en sa vigueur, c'est de ne pas consentir à ses effets et de retenir plusieurs des mouvements auxquels elle dispose le corps. Par exemple, si la colère fait lever la main pour frapper, la volonté peut ordinairement la retenir, ...[55]

The will has a power of veto, therefore, which prevents the force of passions from issuing in any action. Besides, on Descartes's view, the passions in themselves are equally susceptible of being directed to either good or bad ends, and are thus morally indifferent. In an article in the same treatise, entitled "Quel est le mouvement des esprits en ces passions", he writes

---

[53] L. 148; B. 425. Pascal endorses here the Thomist view both that man's will is necessarily set toward his final good, possession of which brings happiness, and that it is under the impulse of this innate orientation of the will that all particular choices are made. Cf. Thomas Aquinas, *Summa Theologica,* 1ª, II ᵃᵉ, Q. 13, a. 6. *Summa Contra Gentiles,* III, 3. E. Rolland, *La loi de réalisation humaine dans Saint Thomas,* Paris 1935, pp. 18-23.

[54] Cf. L. 661; B. 81: "L'esprit croit naturellement, et la volonté aime naturellement; de sorte que, faute de vrais objets, il faut qu'ils s'attachent aux faux." For Saint Augustine's similar conception of the way the will directs men's acts along the line of their dominant desire see E. Gilson, *Introduction à l'étude de Saint Augustin,* p. 174, n. 2.

[55] *Œuvres et lettres,* ed. Bridoux, p. 718.

... je ne vois point de raison qui empêche que le même mouvement des esprits qui sert à fortifier une pensée lorsqu'elle a un fondement qui est mauvais, ne la puisse aussi fortifier lorsqu'elle en a un qui est juste; ...[56]

Indeed the utility of the passions consists essentially in the way they help to strengthen intellectual conviction. And Descartes also argues that if the enquiry is limited to the physiological level the passions appear for the most part geared to meet man's physical needs and therefore beneficial. In short

... nous voyons qu'elles sont toutes bonnes de leur nature, et que nous n'avons rien à éviter que leurs mauvais usages ou leurs excès, ...[57]

Thomas Aquinas likewise regards the passions as in themselves morally indifferent: when in accordance with right reason and subject to its control they are good, but when allowed to obscure reason they are bad.[58] Should they anticipate the action of the will however, even if they make for the good, their influence is injurious and detracts from the moral quality of the act. On the other hand they may be called into existence and used by the will, and in this situation the passions will increase the goodness of the act.[59]

To Pascal the passions, far from being morally indifferent or liable to reason, are enemies of true morality, obstacles to faith and the cause of man's alienation from God.[60] Like Nicole, Pascal believes that instead of ordering his life by reason, as the philosophers hold, man

... ne se conduit que par la passion qui le domine: ...[61]
... Nous flottons dans la mer de ce monde au gré de nos passions, qui nous emportent ... Souvent même la raison n'est pas corrompuë. Elle voit ce qu'il faudroit faire, et elle est convaincuë du néant des choses qui nous agitent; mais elle ne sçauroit empêcher l'impression violente qu'elles font sur nous.[62]

The Augustinian conception of man's enslavement to concupiscence since the Fall accounts for the tendency on the part of the will to give in to pressure from the passions, which seem to lead to happiness when they lead away from it.

---

[56] *Ibid.*, p. 772.
[57] *Ibid.*, p. 794.
[58] *Summa Theologica*, Iᵃ IIᵃᵉ, Q. 14, a. 2; Q. 59, a. 2.
[59] *De Veritate*, Q. 26, a. 7. Cf. A.-D. Sertillanges, *La philosophie morale de Saint Thomas D'Aquin*, pp. 68-72. K. E. Kirk, *The Vision of God: The Christian Doctrine of the Summum Bonum*, London 1931, p. 384, n. 2.
[60] L. 418; B. 233. L. 433; B. 783, L. 260; B. 678. L. 502; B. 571.
[61] *Essais de morale*, vol. II, new ed., Paris 1693, p. 370.
[62] *Essais de morale*, vol. I. 6th ed., Paris 1682, p. 53.

La concupiscence nous est devenue naturelle, et a fait notre seconde nature. Ainsi il y a deux natures en nous: l'une bonne, l'autre mauvaise.[63]
La concupiscence et la force sout les sources de toutes nos actions: la concupiscence fait les volontaires; ...[64]
...la concupiscence est la source de tous nos mouvements; ...[65]
...la malice de la concupiscence se plaît à faire tout le contraire de ce qu'on veut obtenir de nous sans nous donner du plaisir, qui est la monnaie pour laquelle nous donnons tout ce qu'on veut.[66]

Concupiscence is therefore a rival with man's natural desire for happiness as his dominant motive. And, as earlier fragments showed, Pascal believes it frequently hoodwinks the will into choosing mere pleasure as the object of pursuit instead of true happiness. In the *De l'art de persuader* he insists that the act of volition should follow on the recognition by the intellect that something is congenial to man's happiness and therefore desirable. The fact that in practice the passions govern the process of volition, so that the will makes its choice independently of the intellect, is a sign of disorder. The intellect is reduced to merely claiming that it should be "juge des choses que la volonté choisit", while the will, through its "sales attachements", has become totally corrupt.[67] Thus

...bien peu [de vérités] entrent [dans l'âme] par l'esprit, au lieu qu'elles y sont introduites en foule par les caprices téméraires de la volonté, sans le conseil du raisonnement.[68]

The way in which concupiscence, the cause of this disorder, seduces the will from the proper path to consummate happiness, which in Pascal's eyes represents man's end, is made plain in the *Deuxième écrit sur la grâce*.

La concupiscence s'est donc élevée dans ses membres et a chatouillé et délecté sa volonté dans le mal, et les ténèbres ont rempli son esprit de telle sorte que sa volonté, auparavant indifférente pour le bien et le mal, sans délectation ni chatouillement ni dans l'un ni dans l'autre, mais suivant, sans aucun appétit prévenant de sa part, ce qu'il connaissait de plus convenable à sa félicité, se trouve maintenant charmée par la concupiscence ...[69]

It follows from this, according to Pascal, that free will, though retaining its power of choice, nevertheless

---

[63] L. 616; B. 660. Cf. L. 149; B. 430.
[64] L. 97; B. 334.
[65] L. 798; B. 41.
[66] L. 710; B. 24.
[67] C. p. 592; G.E. IX, p. 272.
[68] C. p. 593; G.E. IX, p. 273.
[69] C. p. 965; G.E. XI, p. 147.

... a une suavité et une délectation si puissante dans le mal par la concupiscence qu'infailliblement il s'y porte de lui-même comme à son bien, et qu'il le choisit volontairement et très librement et avec joie comme l'objet où il sent sa béatitude.[70]

Pascal follows the tradition of scholastic psychology here when he describes the proper function of the will as leading man to choose and take to himself something which the intelligence has presented to him as good.[71] This means that his reason for condemning the misuse of the power of thought is not simply that those who apply themselves to illusory pleasures and frivolous pastimes disregard what is for him the fundamental principle of ethics. More serious than this, they are guilty of conniving at deluding the will, already distorted by concupiscence, in presenting to it, as congenial to the supreme desire for happiness, objects which are really obstacles to its attainment.

Pascal seems caught in something of a cleft stick here. On the one hand he is committed, by the Augustinian doctrine of original sin, to the view that the tyranny of concupiscence over the will prevents the intellect ensuring that human acts are directed to their true goal. Indeed the mind itself is no longer a reliable guide since its vision has been clouded by the Fall too, and it has become clogged by sense images. But this makes nonsense of the measure of self-determination, and of control over the will, which Pascal apparently recognizes in the mind when he emphasizes man's duty to order his thinking correctly, so that the intellect will play its proper part in determining the morality of his acts.[72] The difficulty seems almost inescapable for the Augustinian theologian who attempts to preserve human moral responsibility, while at the same time making man entirely dependent upon divine grace for any power to do good.[73] Far from offering any real solution to the problem, Pascal, if anything, underlines it by applying in addition his own doctrine of the three orders to moral questions.

---

[70] C. p. 966; G.E. XI, p. 148.

[71] It is clear that Pascal's "will" is properly the scholastic intellectual appetite, by which man desires a good consciously apprehended by the intelligence. For the Schoolmen the primary function of the will is "electio", by which man recognizes, and takes to himself as his good, what his intelligence has already represented as desirable. Cf. P. H. Wicksteed, *The Reactions between Dogma and Philosophy Illustrated from the Works of S. Thomas Aquinas*, London 1920, Excursus I, pp. 582-620. According to Pascal, however, the will has become so enthralled by concupiscence since the Fall that all conscious choice is excluded from its scope, so that the resultant action does not follow upon the 'election' of what the judgement has presented as good.

[72] Cf. above, pp. 64 ff.

[73] Cf. N. P. Williams, *The Grace of God*, pp. 28-30, 39-41, and *The Ideas of the Fall and of Original Sin*, pp. 368-371.

Jean Domat, Pascal's friend and colleague, illustrates the same inconsistency when he tries to do justice both to the tradition of Augustinian theology, with its emphasis on man's fallen nature, and to the tradition of the natural law school of jurists. The two streams run through his writings side by side with no real bridge between them. Thus in his *Harangues* Domat insists continually that the natural principles of equity are indelibly inscribed in man's reason, so that it is impossible for him not to know them.[74] Even the pagans, he maintains, acknowledge fundamental principles of natural law like the golden rule, since "pour connoître la justice il ne faut que la lumière du bon sens".[75] These truths, as Domat calls them, confront the mind in such a clear, pure and consistent light that they produce immediate conviction.[76]

However, Domat is equally emphatic in the *Harangues* that man in his present state is naturally biassed to evil. All men, he alleges, are born unjust, and this injustice has its seat in the intellect and will, the very faculties on which God imprinted natural law. As a source of injustice these are now said to be of "malheureuse et inconcevable fécondité." [77] In the aftermath of the Fall the understanding, which should be enlightened by truth and justice, has become blind and prejudiced; while the will, which should be motivated by love of truth and justice, has become enslaved to vice through its bias to evil.[78] There seems little scope left here for the play of the natural light of reason!

Even if the understanding had escaped the Fall unscathed it would still be helpless to implement natural law because of the peculiar relation in which it stands to the will. Although it is the function of the intellect to represent an object as a good to the will for it to choose, nevertheless "la volonté est toujours la maîtresse". For, as Domat puts it, knowledge is useless if the will, which is the principle of action, refuses to act! [79] On the other hand the intellect follows infallibly after the will's dominant impulse. Even that delight, therefore, which Domat pictures the mind taking in the truth, its natural object, is powerless to counteract the will when it uses the mind to secure its own criminal ends.[80]

---

[74] *Harangue prononcée aux Assises de l'année 1682*, in *Les loix civiles dans leur ordre naturel*, new ed., Paris 1735, t. II, p. 285, col. 1. Cf. *Harangue . . . 1677*, p. 276, col. 1; *Harangue . . . 1679*, p. 281, col. 1; *Traité des Loix*, chap. I. ibid., t. I, pp. i-ii, chap. IX, p.xi, col. 1-2.

[75] *Harangue . . . 1673*, p. 270, col. 1. Cf. *Harangue . . . 1672*, p. 268, col. 2.

[76] *Harangue . . . 1657*, p. 247, col. 1-2, p. 248, col. 2.

[77] *Harangue . . . 1675*, p. 273, col. 2. Cf. *Le Droit Public*, ibid., p. 3, col. 1.

[78] *Ibid.*

[79] *Harangue . . . 1675*, p. 274, col. 1.

[80] *Ibid.*

...de sorte que dans ces occasions, l'entendement n'est plus que comme un instrument esclave d'un Tyran aveugle.[81]

From this state of slavery the understanding can be released only if God intervenes to raise the will to the good and so overcome man's "pente naturelle au mal".[82]

For Nicole, who does not have the same interest as Pascal and Domat in trying to preserve the integrity of reason, a more ready solution to the problem of the interaction of reason and will is to hand. He represents reason as being persuaded to become, knowingly, a partner in crime as it were. Like Pascal and Domat he believes the will needs to be activated by having the intellect present something to it as a good to be appropriated. Men cannot help therefore to some extent acting in accordance with reason.[83] While pleasure may induce them to do things that run counter to the dictates of reason, a state of tension between the passions and the intellect is insupportable. Agreement between the two sides of human nature must be reached, and in order to satisfy both intellect and will, reason and the passions

...ils font ensorte que leur raison, se rendant flexible à leurs inclinations, se forme des maximes de conduite qui y sont conformes, et selon lesquelles elle peut approuver leurs actions. Ainsi ils établissent la paix en eux-mêmes, par cette mutuelle correspondance de leurs actions et de leurs maximes. Ils pensent comme ils agissent, et ils agissent comme ils pensent: et ils n'ont garde de se condamner eux-mêmes, puisque leur volonté suit toûjours ce que l'esprit luy prescrit, et que l'esprit prescrit toûjours à leur volonté ce qu'elle désire.[84]

The solution Nicole proposes here will only work of course if intellect and will are looked upon as separate things having independent existence, but subject to the control of a kind of 'third man'. Indeed, according to the psychology of all three writers, it is hardly an exaggeration to describe man as made up of a number of subordinate beings called will, reason and so forth, all jostling to determine which will take precedence of the others.

Pascal's assertion, that when man's will is led astray by concupiscence from the pursuit of what is "convenable à sa félicité" his conduct becomes evil, implies that in his view right conduct is the pursuit of true happiness, when the will is duly set in the way of its final end. However, in the Deuxième écrit sur la grâce he goes on to affirm that the only remedy to the domination of the will by concupiscence, the sole means

---

[81] *Ibid.*
[82] *Harangue,...1672*, p. 266, col. 1. Cf. p. 265, col. 1-2.
[83] *Essais de morale*, vol. II, p. 7.
[84] *Ibid.*, p. 8.

of redirecting it toward objects which do lead to happiness, is the grace of Christ. He describes this grace as

... [elle] n'est autre chose qu'une suavité et une délectation dans la loi de Dieu, répandue dans le cœur par le Saint-Esprit, qui non seulement égalant, mais surpassant encore la concupiscence de la chair, remplit la volonté d'une plus grande délectation dans le bien, que la concupiscence ne lui en offre dans le mal, et qu'ainsi le libre arbitre, charmé par les douceurs et par les plaisirs que le Saint-Esprit lui inspire, plus que par les attraits du péché, choisit infailliblement lui-même la loi de Dieu par cette seule raison qu'il y trouve plus de satisfaction et qu'il y sent sa béatitude et sa félicité.[85]

Thus even the operation of divine grace takes the form of a 'delectation' of the will, by means of which it is released from its perverse attachments and is redirected to the pursuit of man's true goal. Pascal follows Saint Augustine here when he both equates grace with the Holy Spirit, and describes it as a kind of gift which must therefore be separate from the Holy Spirit.[86] And in order to preserve an appearance of freedom in the will, while at the same time emphasizing the irresistible quality of grace, Pascal, as N. P. Williams has said of Saint Augustine, "is driven to make use of shifts and expedients which ... it is difficult to regard as more than mere verbal jugglery." [87] The passage certainly implies that man's

---

[85] C. pp. 966-7; G.E. XI, pp. 148-9. The substance of this passage is derived from *De Spiritu et Littera*, 5, where Saint Augustine sums up his teaching on the "delectatio iustitiae". Cf. N. P. Williams, *The Grace of God*, p. 25, and J. Burnaby, *Amor Dei*, pp. 220-3. Saint Augustine adopts the same view in *De Peccatorum Meritis et Remissione*, II, 26. "Men are unwilling to do what is just and right, either because it is unknown to them, or because it is unpleasant to them. For we have the stronger desire for a thing, in proportion to the certainty of our knowledge how good it is, and in proportion to the warmth of satisfaction which that knowledge occasions. Ignorance, therefore, and infirmity are faults which hinder our will from moving either to the performance of a good work, or to the refraining from an evil one. But in order that what was hidden may come to light, and what was unpleasant may become agreeable, the grace of God operates and assists the wills of men." *The Anti-Pelagian Works of Saint Augustine*, translated by Peter Holmes, Edinburgh 1872, vol. I, pp. 98-9. Pascal also follows Saint Augustine's belief that because of the enslavement of his will man's actions are determined by what delights him most. In the *Troisième écrit sur la grâce* he quotes Augustine's statement "Quod amplius delectat, secundum id operemur necesse est." *(Exp. Ep. ad Gal.,* 49), and alleges that man is "maintenant esclave de la délectation; ce qui le délecte davantage l'attire infailliblement: ... l'on fait toujours ce qui délecte le plus." C. p. 1003; G.E. XI, p. 226.

[86] Cf. N. P. Williams, *The Grace of God*, pp. 25-6.

[87] *The Ideas of the Fall and of Original Sin*, p. 368. Commenting elsewhere on statements by Saint Augustine which show quite unmistakably that, despite disclaimers, he regards grace as irresistible, Williams writes: "There is no struggling against a force which represents all the might of omnipotence, directed by all the intellectual resources of omniscience. God is in the position of a chess-player, gifted with telepathic and hypnotic power of an infinitely high degree, who not merely foresees all the other player's moves, but actually makes them, acting

own unaided efforts to progress toward the goal of his desires, to perform good acts, will be of no avail in the face of a will enthralled by concupiscence.[88] As Martineau put it, referring to the moral implications of Augustinian theology, on this view "man ... as an ethical agent sinks into nonentity, and becomes the mere prize contended for by the spirits of darkness and of light." [89] Since the powers of concupiscence and grace are conceived of as rival delectations, the will becomes a sort of mechanical reflex actuated by whichever delectation happens to be strongest. In such circumstances no moral responsibility can be imputed to it. David Hume, in his discussion of liberty and necessity, puts his finger on the difficulty that confronts Pascal here in his typically Augustinian insistence on man's state of absolute dependence: "... as a man who fired a train is answerable for all the consequences, whether the train he employed be long or short; so, wherever a continued chain of necessary causes is fixed, that Being, either finite or infinite, who produces the first, is likewise the author of all the rest, and must both bear the blame and acquire the praise which belong to them." [90]

Although he implies that left to himself man is incapable of moral endeavour, Pascal does not hesitate to derive a concept of duty from the natural desire for happiness. He argues that this fundamental impulse and capacity determine in advance what the true religion must reveal to man about his nature, ground and end.

Il faut que, pour rendre l'homme heureux, elle lui montre qu'il y a un Dieu; qu'on est obligé de l'aimer; que notre unique félicité est d'être en lui, et notre unique mal d'être séparé de lui; qu'elle reconnaisse que nous sommes pleins de

through the other's brain, and who consequently has won the game before it has even begun." *The Grace of God*, p. 28. A typical example of Pascal's "verbal jugglery" occurs in the *Prière pour le bon usage des maladies:* "Oh! qu'heureux sont ceux qui avec une liberté entière et une pente invincible de leur volonté aiment parfaitement et librement ce qu'ils sont obligés d'aimer nécessairement!" C. p. 609; G.E. IX, p. 329. The description in the 18th *Provinciale* of the action of divine grace on the human will concludes on the same note: "... trouvant sa plus grande joie dans le Dieu qui le charme, [l'homme] s'y porte infailliblement de lui-même, par un mouvement tout libre, tout volontaire, tout amoureux; ..." C. p. 887; G.E. VII, p. 29.

[88] Cf. also the cryptic but telling assertions in the *Pensées:* "... toute la morale [consiste] en la concupiscence et en la grâce." L. 226; B. 523. "... [Dieu] donne dans la morale la charité, qui produit des fruits contre la concupiscence." L. 536; B. 579.

[89] *Types of Ethical Theory*, 2nd ed., Oxford 1886, vol. I, p. 18. Cf. Professor Jan Miel's discussion of Pascal's treatment of the relation between grace and free will in *Pascal and Theology*, pp. 98-104.

[90] *An Enquiry Concerning Human Understanding*, Section VIII, Part II, in Hume: *Theory of Knowledge*, ed. D. C. Yalden-Thomson, London 1951, p. 103.

ténèbres qui nous empêchent de le connaître et de l'aimer; et qu'ainsi nos devoirs nous obligeant d'aimer Dieu, et nos concupiscences nous en détournant,...[91]

Man has a duty to love God, therefore, not because of a moral law that commands him to, but because in God alone can he find the full satisfaction of his whole nature. An earlier variant of another part of the same fragment also illustrates this Augustinian practice of making the moral quality of any action depend directly on its relation to God as the supreme good for man.

Ne cherchez pas de satisfaction dans la terre: ... Votre bien n'est qu'en Dieu, et la souveraine félicité consiste à connaître Dieu, à s'unir à lui pour jamais dans l'éternité. Votre devoir est à l'aimer de tout votre cœur.[92]

That man is powerless to carry out this duty by himself does not seem to detract from its binding force in Pascal's view. He insists, not merely that men can or will love God through the agency of grace, but, less intelligibly, that they have a duty to do so. The conclusion, however, is inescapable that actions induced in this way for duty's sake are devoid of moral quality, since clearly no merit or blame can attach to an act which a man cannot help performing.

A further fragment from the *Pensées* shows how Pascal sets up man's supreme good or end as the moral criterion, assigning the labels good and bad to human acts and finite objects of desire according as they tend to promote or hinder the attainment of the ultimate goal.

Or, la dernière fin est ce qui donne le nom aux choses. Tout ce qui nous empêche d'y arriver est appelé ennemi. Ainsi les créatures, quoique bonnes, sont ennemies des justes quand elles les détournent de Dieu,...[93]

[91] L. 149; B. 430. The process by which Thomas Aquinas arrives at an a priori definition of the conditions with which an authentic revelation must comply, although more complex than Pascal's, is basically the same. Revelation must make available the supplementary information both about the ultimate goal where man's natural desire for blessedness will find fulfilment, and about the means for attaining it, which his own unaided faculties cannot provide. *Summa Theologica*, I[a], Q. 1, a. 1. *Summa Contra Gentiles*, III, 118. Cf. P. H. Wicksteed, *op. cit.*, pp. 154-6.

[92] C. p. 1225; B. 430. Cf. Saint Augustine, *De Moribus Ecclesiae Catholicae*, 14. As Jean Laporte puts it in his account of Arnauld's views on this point, "le commandement d'aimer Dieu nous prescrit non pas d'aimer quelque chose qui nous est peut-être indifférent, mais d'actualiser, de réaliser de façon réfléchie, notre instinct naturel, de faire explicitement ce que nous faisons tous implicitement en vertu de notre nature, d'aller d'un mouvement et libre et consenti dans le sens où va la nécessité de notre nature." *La doctrine de Port-Royal*, vol. III, *La morale d'après Arnauld*, p. 102.

[93] L. 502; B. 571. M. Gilson has shown how this conception of the 'end', as identified with the sovereign good, God, distinguishes the specifically Christian ethic from that propounded by the ancient philosophers, who also conceived of the 'end' as determining morals. He points out that for Aristotle the 'end' is not something which transcends and completes the moral life: the sole 'end' and true

Thus in a particular context certain things or acts will be condemned as bad or wrong, not because they are necessarily bad or wrong in themselves, but because they will clearly deter man from achieving his true good. Action, therefore, should be governed by determining the right means to the goal of man's desires. Like Arnauld and Nicole, Pascal adopts the scholastic view that only if all his conduct is adapted to attaining the end will every act a man performs be in some measure effectively good.[94] And not only do human acts derive their moral quality from their relation to man's final end, but Pascal believes that finite things themselves should be judged by their tendency to promote this ultimate good of man.

Indeed the two are inextricably bound up for, according to Pascal's psychology, it is the desire or love of some thing that dictates all man's motives, which are in turn effective in shaping his actual behaviour. The need for grace to exercise a superior delectation, in order to free man from his enslavement to concupiscence, brought this out plainly enough.[95] Right conduct for Pascal consists then simply in keeping to

good is the moral life itself. *L'esprit de la philosophie médiévale,* pp. 336 ff. The practice of declaring human acts and objects of desire morally good or bad in so far as they are compatible or not with the attainment of man's final 'end' seems to have been generally adopted by Jansenist writers. Arnauld, echoing Saint Augustine, maintains that: "... la principale distinction des vertus d'avec les vices, et des bonnes actions d'avec les péchés, se doit prendre de la fin à laquelle elles doivent être rapportées, et cette fin n'est autre que Dieu,..." *Seconde apologie pour Monsieur Jansénius, Oeuvres,* Paris 1777, t. XVII, p. 342. Nicole likewise asserts: "... la Religion est si étroitement liée à toutes les choses du monde, par le rapport qu'elles ont à la fin dernière qui est Dieu, que l'on ne sçauroit juger d'aucune que par ce rapport. C'est par là qu'elles sont avantageuses, désavantageuses, innocentes ou dangereuses, estimables, méprisables, bonnes ou mauvaises. Le prix qu'elles ont en elles-mêmes n'est rien. Elles l'empruntent tout du rapport qu'elles ont au souverain bien." *Essais de morale,* vol. II, pp. 64-5. Jansenius himself insists on the importance, as far as virtue is concerned, of duly differentiating between "officium" and "finis", between the act itself and the 'end' which the agent has in view in performing it. According to him the essential difference between vice and virtue lies not in the action considered in itself, but in the 'end' which alone 'specifies' the action and makes it what it is. It is the 'end' that determines the will, thus motivating the action; and man's final 'end', to which all his acts must be referred, is God. *Augustinus,* t. II, bk. IV, ch. 12. Despite the different connotation which the term itself bears in his case, Descartes too considers that the 'end' should rightly determine conduct. In his letter to Elisabeth, 18.8.1645, he notes: "... la dernière fin ou le but auquel doivent tendre nos actions: ... par la fin de nos actions, on peut entendre [le souverain bien et la béatitude]; car le souverain bien est sans doute la chose que nous nous devons proposer pour but en toutes nos actions, et le contentement d'esprit qui en revient, étant l'attrait qui fait que nous le recherchons, est aussi à bon droit nommé notre fin." *Œuvres et lettres,* ed. Bridoux, p. 1198.

⁹⁴ Cf. J. Laporte, *La morale d'après Arnauld,* p. 113. Nicole, *Essais de morale,* vol. IV, p. 385.

⁹⁵ Cf. *De l'art de persuader,* "... aussitôt qu'on fait apercevoir à l'âme qu'une

right desires; to those which encourage the pursuit of what can alone supply the need of man's nature. A passage from the *Pensées* illustrates the conclusion to which this argument leads.

S'il y a un Dieu, il ne faut aimer que lui, et non les créatures passagères. ... Donc tout ce qui nous incite à nous attacher aux créatures est mauvais, puisque cela nous empêche, ou de servir Dieu, si nous le connaissons, ou de le chercher, si nous l'ignorons.[96]

Pascal shares with Nicole a suspicion of personal attachments for the same reason that they are apt to divert men's desires from the proper end where they will find satisfaction.

Il est injuste qu'on s'attache à moi, quoiqu'on le fasse avec plaisir et volontairement. Je tromperais ceux à qui j'en ferais naître le désir, car je ne suis la fin de personne et n'ai pas de quoi les satisfaire.[97]

As Pascal sees it, no finite being can be the end of any other finite being because such a being is, by definition, incapable of satisfying the desire for an infinite good that characterizes human nature. And to get things so far out of perspective as to allow finite objects to usurp the rank of final end of one's desires amounts, in his opinion, to sacrilege. In an early letter to Mme Périer he refers to created things in these terms.

... l'on voit que dans les ténèbres du monde on les suit par un aveuglement brutal, que l'on s'y attache et qu'on en fait la dernière fin de ses désirs, ce qu'on ne peut faire sans sacrilège, car il n'y a que Dieu qui doive être la dernière fin comme lui seul est le vrai principe.[98]

Pascal, as has been shown, believes that men fail to direct their acts toward the true end because they tend to give in to the desire which happens to be uppermost at the moment, but whose satisfaction leads away from the goal. This capitulation is in turn caused by the monopoly which concupiscence has over man's will. And at the end of the fragment urging man's duty to love God rather than mere creatures, Pascal deduces a further duty binding upon men in this situation.

Or nous sommes pleins de concupiscence: donc nous sommes pleins de mal; donc nous devons nous haïr nous-mêmes, et tout ce qui nous excite à autre attache qu'à Dieu seul.[99]

chose peut la conduire à ce qu'elle aime souverainement, il est inévitable qu'elle ne s'y porte avec joie." C. p. 594; G.E. IX, p. 274. Pascal again adopts the Augustinian approach to this question. Cf. E. Gilson, *Introduction à l'étude de Saint Augustin*, pp. 174-7.

[96] L. 618; B. 479.
[97] L. 396; B. 471. Cf. Nicole, *Essais de morale*, vol. II, pp. 128-136.
[98] C. pp. 484-5; G.E. II, p. 250.
[99] L. 618; B. 479.

Similar recommendations occur elsewhere in the *Pensées*.

La vraie et unique vertu est donc de se haïr (car on est haïssable par sa concupiscence), et de chercher un être véritablement aimable, pour l'aimer.[100]
Qui ne hait en soi son amour-propre, et cet instinct qui le porte à se faire Dieu,
est bien aveuglé.[101]
Il y en a qui voient bien qu'il n'y a pas d'autre ennemi de l'homme que la concupiscence, qui le détourne de Dieu,... ni d'autre bien que Dieu,... Ceux qui
croient que le bien de l'homme est en la chair, et le mal en ce qui le détourne des
plaisirs des sens, qu'il s'en soûle et qu'il y meure.[102]

But when he advocates self-hatred in this way, as the proper channel for
moral effort and the source of true virtue, Pascal does not alter the basic
direction of his ethics. It is precisely in man's own ultimate interest, as
furthering his pursuit of happiness, to redress by this means the balance
upset by the enslavement of his impulses to concupiscence. Human
nature, as the result of its corruption by the Fall, has become the seat of
concupiscence, which sets up as objects of pursuit what are really obstacles to be overcome if man is to attain his sovereign good. This is clear
from the form concupiscence usually takes: the stimulus of the flesh
that induces men to seek pleasure for its own sake as the supreme goal,
and a tendency on the part of the individual to treat himself as God,
seeking the ultimate satisfaction of his desires in his own finite nature.
To indulge either of these inclinations is, in Pascal's terms, to be led
astray from the true path to the final end, and so to leave unfulfilled the
supreme desire for happiness which controls even such false choices as
these.

As a corollary of the view that things and acts are good or bad
according as they tend to help or hinder man's progress toward his final
goal, Pascal believes that to perform good actions, and so ultimately
achieve perfect happiness, the individual must act from the motive of
conforming to the divine will. To treat God as his final end, and as the
source of all good, requires the individual to submit his will to the will
of God. Thus in the *Pensées* Pascal urges

Changeons la règle que nous avons prise jusqu'ici pour juger de ce qui est bon.
Nous en avions pour règle notre volonté, prenons maintenant la volonté de Dieu:
tout ce qu'il veut nous est bon et juste, ...[103]

And in the fifth letter addressed to Mlle de Roannez he writes

---

[100] L. 564; B. 485.
[101] L. 617; B. 492.
[102] L. 269; B. 692.
[103] L. 948; B. 668.

Il est temps de commencer à juger de ce qui est bon ou mauvais par la volonté de Dieu, qui ne peut être ni injuste ni aveugle, et non pas par la nôtre propre, qui est toujours pleine de malice et d'erreur.[104]

The same point is made in another fragment from the *Pensées*, introduced under the rubric *"Morale"*, where he develops the theory of the "membres pensants". Pascal uses the terms "âme universelle", "âme entière", here to denote God as the ultimate source of all derived existence, and alleges that it is a pre-condition of happiness for individual members that they have "bonne volonté pour consentir à celle de l'âme universelle", and that

... leur béatitude, aussi bien que leur devoir, consistant à consentir à la conduite de l'âme entière à qui ils appartiennent, ...[105]

In much of his adverse criticism of the modes of life and thought adopted by his contemporaries Pascal clearly uses as criterion of judgement his own belief that all the individual's actions should be affiliated to the supreme goal of his desires, and that his whole life should be ordered to the eternal felicity to which the promise of his nature points. The great danger, as it seems to Pascal, that confronts men in their present fallen condition is cryptically outlined in the following fragment.

La vraie nature étant perdue, tout devient sa nature; comme le véritable bien étant perdu, tout devient son véritable bien.[106]

Men are tempted, therefore, to accept the actual state of their nature as the true one, and, having lost sight of the true good, to replace it with whatever finite object happens to come to hand. If yielded to, this line of action will lead to abandoning all moral effort. Consequently Pascal is concerned in his judgements, not so much with the various activities themselves, which absorb men's attention, as with the attitude of mind behind them and the factors determining it.

It is for this reason that he deplores the control exercised by the 'imagination' over the rest of man's faculties.

Je rapporterais presque toutes les actions des hommes qui ne branlent presque que par ses secousses. Car la raison a été obligée de céder, et la plus sage prend pour ses principes ceux que l'imagination des hommes a témérairement introduits en chaque lieu. ... Il faut, parce qu'il lui a plu, travailler tout le jour pour des biens reconnus pour imaginaires; et quand le sommeil nous a délassés des fatigues de notre raison, il faut incontinent se lever en sursaut pour aller courir après les fumées et essuyer les impressions de cette maîtresse du monde. – Voilà un des principes d'erreur, ...[107]

[104] C. p. 511; G.E. VI, p. 159. Cf. C. p. 508; G.E. VI, p. 84.
[105] L. 360; B. 482.
[106] L. 397; B. 426.
[107] L. 44; B. 82.

When Pascal labels the imagination here "un des principes d'erreur", he does not refer to the fact that the deception it practises is intermittent, so that it cannot be accepted as a reliable guide to either truth or falsehood. What he has in mind is the way in which it positively leads men astray, by deluding them about the value of the ends they pursue. Its subjugation of reason, together with the monopoly it holds of the springs of action, results in a general incapacity to perceive the vanity of human existence. And the futile particulars ("des biens imaginaires"), which engross the attention while men are under its sway, must crowd out all thought of their supernatural destiny, and so finally blur their sense of the true character of the final goal.

For the same reason Pascal considers the influence which 'habit' exerts in determining men to a particular line of conduct morally pernicious.

La prévention induisant en erreur. – C'est une chose déplorable de voir tous les hommes ne délibérer que des moyens, et point de la fin. Chacun songe comme il s'acquittera de sa condition; mais pour le choix de la condition, et de la patrie, le sort nous le donne. C'est une chose pitoyable, de voir tant de Turcs, d'hérétiques, d'infidèles, suivre le train de leurs pères, par cette seule raison qu'ils ont été prévenus chacun que c'est le meilleur. . . .[108]

Thus, in what Pascal regards as their most far-reaching decisions, men allow themselves to be guided simply by what they are used to. Social tradition and environment even determine their belief about the possibility and nature of the final end to which their whole life should be directed. And the adjectives "déplorable" and "pitoyable", used to describe the state things have come to when men permit themselves to shut out of sight in this way the bearing of the end on all their choices, show plainly enough that it is Pascal's preoccupation with man's otherworldly destiny which determines his judgement here.

But what he believes is above all else responsible for inducing men to turn their back on the things which it should be their first concern to call before their minds, if they are to move toward their end, is the dread of what they will find if they do so. It is to avoid this, Pascal maintains, that men give themselves over to those pastimes which he calls "divertissement" in the Pensées. His own reaction to this sort of attitude is well illustrated in the following fragment.

Misère. – La seule chose qui nous console de nos misères est le divertissement, et cependant c'est la plus grande de nos misères. Car c'est cela qui nous empêche principalement de songer à nous. . . . Sans cela, nous serions dans l'ennui, et cet

[108] L. 193; B. 98.

ennui nous pousserait à chercher un moyen plus solide d'en sortir. Mais le divertissement nous amuse, et nous fait arriver insensiblement à la mort.[109]

In Pascal's view the real danger in supposing that "divertissement" offers
genuine relief from misery is that, while making men temporarily happy,
it prevents them being compelled by the very consciousness of misery
to take steps to arrive at a permanent solution. As Bishop Butler put
it ". . . the amusements, which men usually pass their time in, are so far
from coming up to or answering our notions and desires of happiness,
or good, that they are really no more than . . . somewhat which serves
to turn us aside from, and prevent our attending to, this our internal
poverty and want; . . ." [110] "Divertissement" lulls men into insensibility,
so that all incentive is lost to take thought about the sort of conduct
which is compatible with the attainment of the goal proper to their
nature. Once again it is Pascal's concern to urge men to regulate their
conduct in accordance with their own ultimate good and final end that
lies at the root of his criticism of "divertissement".

Pascal holds, then, that ethics should be geared primarily to bring men
to find out what course of action is best adjusted for them, in the sense
of leading to their own conclusive happiness. This again becomes apparent when he censures those who pride themselves on having shaken
off the yoke, and who now affect complete indifference to Christian
doctrines relating to their own destiny. In his view such behaviour is
not merely irrational and irresponsible,[111] but is totally lacking in regard
for their own interests also.[112] The argument which he repeatedly ad-
vances to convict this sort of conduct of extravagance runs as follows:

. . . il est indubitable que le temps de cette vie n'est qu'un instant, que l'état de
la mort est éternel, de quelque nature qu'il puisse être, et qu'ainsi toutes nos
actions et nos pensées doivent prendre des routes si différentes selon l'état de cette

---

[109] L. 414; B. 171.

[110] *Fifteen Sermons Preached at the Rolls Chapel*, ed. W. R. Matthews, London
1914, p. 222.

[111] Pascal even goes so far as to condemn this nonchalant attitude as unnatural.
Thus he maintains that: "De tous leurs égarements, c'est sans doute celui qui les
convainc le plus de folie et d'aveuglement, et dans lequel il est le plus facile de les
confondre par les premières vues du sens commun et par les sentiments de la
nature." L. 428; B. 195. Cf. also L. 427; B. 194.

[112] ". . . cette négligence n'est pas supportable. Il ne s'agit pas ici de l'intérêt
léger de quelque personne étrangère, . . . il s'agit de nous-mêmes, et de notre tout."
L. 427; B. 194. "Cette négligence en une affaire où il s'agit d'eux-mêmes, de leur
éternité, de leur tout, m'irrite plus qu'elle ne m'attendrit; . . . Je ne dis pas ceci par
le zèle pieux d'une dévotion spirituelle. J'entends au contraire qu'on doit avoir ce
sentiment par un principe d'intérêt humain et par un intérêt d'amour-propre: il ne
faut pour cela que voir ce que voient les personnes les moins éclairées." *ibid.*

éternité, qu'il est impossible de faire une démarche avec sens et jugement qu'en la réglant par la vue de ce point qui doit être notre dernier objet.

. . . Que l'on juge donc là-dessus de ceux qui vivent sans songer à cette dernière fin de la vie, . . .[113]

The whole direction of human conduct must depend, therefore, on whether or not there is a future state of existence.[114] These alternatives represent two fundamentally different views of the nature of things, which, so far as he consistently attends to them (and Pascal insists that it is impossible to act reasonably without doing so),[115] must affect the whole of an individual's conduct, and make it quite different in the one case from what it would be in the other. And Pascal's practice of suspending obligation from what men's natural desires show to be their ultimate end, leads to the concurrence in this instance of the moral imperative, which directs the taking of means to this end, and rightly conceived self-interest. Having emphasized the supreme importance of the question he concludes

Ainsi notre premier intérêt et notre premier devoir est de nous éclaircir sur ce sujet, d'où dépend toute notre conduite.[116]

The term "dernière fin" refers in this context to the temporal end of human existence, rather than to its purposive goal. But it is because the attainment of the goal is possible only in a future state that the question of immortality is made to loom so large in determining the direction human acts must take. For, if the present life is all that the individual has to look forward to then his nature, as Pascal depicts it in the *Pensées,* is doomed to miss its mark, and the goal postulated by his infinite desire for happiness is but an illusion. Such is the force of one of the alternative arguments used by Pascal to prove the overriding importance of the issue.

Il est sans doute qu'il n'y a point de bien sans la connaissance de Dieu, qu'à mesure qu'on en approche on est heureux, et que le dernier bonheur est de le connaître avec certitude, qu'à mesure qu'on s'en éloigne on est malheureux, et que le dernier malheur serait la certitude du contraire.[117]

---

[113] L. 428; B. 195.

[114] Another passage very similar to the foregoing makes this even more explicit. "L'immortalité de l'âme est une chose qui nous importe si fort. . . . Toutes nos actions et nos pensées doivent prendre des routes si différentes, selon qu'il y aura des biens éternels à espérer ou non, qu'il est impossible de faire une démarche avec sens . . ." L. 427; B. 194.

[115] Thus the paragraph that follows on directly after "dernier objet" runs: "Il n'y a rien de plus visible que cela et qu'ainsi, selon les principes de la raison, la conduite des hommes est tout à fait déraisonnable, s'ils ne prennent une autre voie." L. 428; B. 195.

[116] L. 427; B. 194.

[117] C. p. 1174; B. 194.

Pascal believes, then, that the problem of immortality should be debated by every human individual because it bears so unquestionably upon the possibility of men attaining the supreme good which will satisfy their desire for happiness.

And it is for this reason too that he is so emphatic that ethics is not, and cannot be, independent of opinions on this question.

Il est indubitable que, que l'âme soit mortelle ou immortelle, cela doit mettre une différence entière dans la morale. Et cependant les philosophes ont conduit leur morale indépendamment de cela: . . .[118]

As the preceding discussion shows, Pascal does not mean by this merely that an individual convinced of his own immortality will attach immeasurably greater importance to the distinction between right and wrong, than one who weighs up the effects of right and wrong actions assuming that the present life is all that he has to look forward to. He is not just trying to make the point that the prospect of future life highlights the importance of every act of moral choice, so that, as Selden put it, "Religion must governe Morallity".[119] The "différence entière", to which Pascal refers, goes deeper and relates to the question: what is right action? For on his view, since the rightness of any act depends on its relation to man's end, the business of ethics is to decide what acts will help man to attain that end, and to prescribe them while discouraging those which would hinder his progress toward it. And the question of immortality bears upon ethics because upon it depends the possibility of the individual attaining his end. To object that it does not make any practical difference to ethics whether there is, or is not, a future life, that right and wrong are quite independent of this hypothesis either way, it would be necessary first to dispose of Pascal's method of deriving the moral imperative from the final end.

The egoistic twist which Pascal gives to traditional teleological morals is most readily apparent in the way he treats this question of immortality. Not that the idea of a future life is any less integral to the scholastic ethical system. The final fruition of the divine aspect, which Thomas Aquinas, for example, considers is alone capable of satisfying the desire of human nature for ultimate blessedness, and which he sets up as the end to which the will should be directed and all action ordered, is impossible for any man in this life. Aquinas was too convinced a follow-

---

[118] L. 612; B. 219. Pascal maintains that failure to take account of this question is enough to disqualify anyone from the title of 'philosopher': "Fausseté des philosophes qui ne discutaient pas l'immortalité de l'âme." L. 409; B. 220.
[119] *Table Talk of John Selden*, ed. Sir Frederick Pollock, p. 83.

er of Aristotle on questions of knowledge ever to allow that human nature by itself has any power of apprehending immaterial things in a direct fashion. The limitations inherent in the conditions of earthly life point to a future state, when God will confer on man powers that lie above and outside his own nature.[120] And since the final end, relation to which determines the moral quality of all acts, is identical with man's supreme good, which can alone give him full and conclusive blessedness, Aquinas is able to dispense with any system of external rewards and punishments. Human actions carry their own sanctions built in as it were, for on this view right acts must necessarily lead to ultimate blessedness, whereas their contraries must tend by effect toward eternal privation of the good.[121]

But Aquinas does not propose the question of a future life with Pascal's almost lurid emphasis on the element of self-interest involved. Nor does he try to bring out its relevance for ethics, as he conceives of them, by dwelling on the eudaemonism implicit in his theory of the good. Unlike Pascal and Nicole,[122] Aquinas does not set out to bring the individual to his senses, by confronting him with a choice between the alternatives of eternal happiness on one hand and everlasting perdition on the other.

---

[120] Cf. extracts quoted by P. H. Wicksteed, *op. cit.*, Excursus II, pp. 644-651.

[121] A.-D. Sertillanges describes in the following terms how, in Thomas Aquinas's view, the 'ultimate' sanctions project into the present: "En ce monde . . . nous ne sommes pas moins reliés à l'éternel par chacun de nos états. Tel de ceux-ci vaut pour notre aboutissement; tel autre pour notre perte; . . . Notre sort se joue à chaque détermination que nous prenons en face de l'absolu qui nous juge. Nous-mêmes, en disant oui ou non au bien, qui est la condition du bonheur, nous prononçons notre jugement." *op. cit.*, p. 579.

[122] Nicole adopts much the same approach as Pascal to the whole question of the bearing of a future life upon the individual's conduct: ". . . ce qu'il y a de plus étonnant et qui fait mieux connoistre que toutes choses l'excès de l'aveuglement des hommes c'est la légèreté prodigieuse avec laquelle ils embrassent les plus importantes maximes de leur conduite, . . . Il s'agit de leur tout, puisqu'il s'agit pour eux d'une éternité de bonheur ou de malheur. Chaque pas qui les avance vers la mort, les approche de l'une ou de l'autre de ces deux éternitez. Ne semble-t-il donc pas que leur principal soin et leur principale application devroit être de s'instruire des règles véritables qu'ils doivent suivre dans la conduite de toute leur vie, et de tâcher de les discerner de ce nombre innombrable de fausses règles qui sont suivies par ceux qui s'éloignent de la vérité." *Essais de morale*, vol. II, pp. 11-12. Cf. *ibid.*, pp. 2-3. "La vie présente par laquelle [l'homme] doit passer, ne luy est donnée que pour faire choix de l'un ou de l'autre de ces deux états [l'Enfer et le Paradis]; et ce choix doit être l'unique employ et l'unique exercice de sa vie. Car il ne se fait pas par une seule action. Elles y contribuent toutes, et servent toutes à l'avancer vers l'un ou vers l'autre." *Essais de morale*, vol. IV, pp. 207-8. Cf. *ibid.*, pp. 4-8, 69-74.

CHAPTER VII

CONCLUSION: MORAL VALUE AS A PERSPECTIVE OF THE THREE ORDERS

The way in which Pascal falls back, when making judgements, on the aspect of things as seen from the supernatural order, combines with his teleological approach to produce a point of view from which all that belongs to this world appears worthless. The pessimistic tone of such passages from the *Pensées* as the following derives from this point of view.

Il ne faut pas avoir l'âme fort élevée pour comprendre qu'il n'y a point ici de satisfaction véritable et solide, que tous nos plaisirs ne sont que vanité... Qu'on fasse réflexion là-dessus et qu'on dise ensuite s'il n'est pas indubitable qu'il n'y a de bien en cette vie qu'en l'espérance d'une autre vie, qu'on n'est heureux qu'à mesure qu'on s'en approche...[1]

By emphasizing in this way the essentially transient quality of human life and worldly goals Pascal is able to show the ultimate good, as he describes it, making even more absolute demands on men. The need for them to order their lives to the pursuit of this true good becomes more imperative when all other goods are made to seem illusory.

Pascal's ready acceptance of the Platonic theme in Augustinian theology contributes further to the tendency to deprive the goods which belong to this world of any ethical character.[2] A letter to Mme Périer

---

[1] L. 427; B. 194. Cf. Saint Augustine, The *City of God*, XIX, 20, Everyman Edition, vol. II, p. 257.

[2] On this aspect of Saint Augustine's thought see E. Gilson, *Introduction à l'étude de Saint Augustin*, pp. 256-274. K. E. Kirk, in his discussion of Saint Augustine's views on the "summum bonum", points out that "The danger of Platonism for the Christian Church has always been that, while it insists that all things depend upon God for their existence, it leaves the reader with vague phrases such as 'shadow', 'copy', 'mirror', as the only light it throws upon the character of that dependence ... it lends itself to a seductive doctrine of the relative worthlessness, the vain and illusory character, of the things of this world, which is very difficult to distinguish from dualism itself, and may have the same practical issue in the depreciation of nature and natural society, ..." *The Vision of God*, p. 329.

contains what Chevalier regards as a virtual paraphrase of the allegory of the shadows in the cave by which Plato illustrates his doctrine of exemplarism in the *The Republic*.

> ... les choses corporelles ne sont qu'une image des spirituelles, et Dieu a représenté les choses invisibles dans les visibles. ... comme nos péchés nous retiennent enveloppés parmi les choses corporelles et terrestres ... il faut que nous nous servions du lieu même où nous sommes tombés pour nous relever de notre chute. C'est pourquoi nous devons bien ménager l'avantage que la bonté de Dieu nous donne de nous laisser toujours devant les yeux une image des biens que nous avons perdus, et de nous environner dans la captivité même où sa justice nous a réduits, de tant d'objets qui nous servent d'une leçon continuellement présente.
>
> De sorte que nous devons nous considérer comme des criminels dans une prison toute remplie des images de leur libérateur et des instructions nécessaires pour sortir de la servitude; ...[3]

Although Chevalier appears to think that when writing this letter Pascal actually had in mind the passage from *The Republic*,[4] it is more probable that he was familiar with the theme as it is developed by Saint Augustine. In *De Vera Religione,* for example, Augustine treats sensible phenomena in a similar fashion as symbols by means of which the mind can rise to contemplate the reality they reflect.[5] And there is a strong likelihood that Pascal was acquainted with this particular work of Saint Augustine since it was translated by Arnauld in 1647, while the letter in question is dated April, 1658.

Pascal adapts to his own purpose the Platonic conception of the physical universe, as a mere reflexion of the world of true reality. The passage implies that by the Fall man lost the capacity of direct vision of supernatural realities, and has had to depend since on the indirect sort of knowledge which can be gleaned from the 'images' that surround him

---

[3] C. p. 484; G.E. II, pp. 249-50.

[4] J. Chevalier, *Pascal,* pp. 80-1.

[5] "... en demeurant attachés au Créateur, qui est éternel, il faut nécessairement que nous participions à l'éternité de sa nature. Mais parce que l'ame étant accablée de ses péchés, et environnée de leurs liens, ne pourroit d'elle-même, ni découvrir, ni conserver cette vérité, s'il n'y avoit quelque degré, par lequel l'homme, s'élevant des choses humaines aux divines, s'efforçât de passer de la vie terrestre à la ressemblance de Dieu même: la Providence éternelle a voulu, par une bonté ineffable, établir, ... des moyens pour secourir les hommes en général et en particulier, en se servant des créatures ... parce que nous naissons ici-bas parmi les choses temporelles, et que leur amour nous empêche d'aimer celles qui sont éternelles, il y a un remede temporel, ... Car en quelque lieu qu'un homme tombe, il faut qu'en ce même endroit il fasse effort pour se relever. Et ainsi, puisque nous avons été si long-temps attachés aux formes corporelles et périssables, nous devons comme nous appuyer sur elles-mêmes, pour nous élever à celles qui sont incorporelles et incorruptibles." *De Vera Religione,* X, 19; XXIV, 45. Antoine Arnauld's translation, contained in *Œuvres de Messire Antoine Arnauld,* t. XI, Paris 1777, pp. 682, 704-5.

on all sides in his state of servitude.[6] The depreciation which the material world undergoes when it is reduced in status in this way to a 'prison-house', filled with mere 'images', needs no emphasis. Not only is it denied any positive value in itself, but its symbolic significance becomes entirely relative. This will depend upon whether the sensible world serves a representative function or tends, instead, to take on the quality of something real and final, attracting to itself the attention which it should direct elsewhere. Pascal goes on in the same letter to condemn such misdirected attention as idolatry.

> ... l'on voit que dans les ténèbres du monde on les suit par un aveuglement brutal, que l'on s'y attache et qu'on en fait la dernière fin de ses désirs, ce qu'on ne peut faire sans sacrilège, car il n'y a que Dieu qui doive être la dernière fin comme lui seul est le vrai principe. Car, quelque ressemblance que la nature créée ait avec son Créateur, et encore que les moindres choses et les plus petites et les plus viles parties du monde représentent au moins par leur unité la parfaite unité qui ne se trouve qu'en Dieu, on ne peut pas légitimement leur porter le souverain respect, parce qu'il n'y a rien de si abominable aux yeux de Dieu et des hommes que l'idolatrie, ...[7]

Man, on Pascal's view, is imprisoned, as the result of the Fall, among the shadows of the world of sensible phenomena, but should be engaged in putting these 'images' to proper use in order to secure release from servitude and gain access to reality. The great danger here is that he tends to forget himself in the process, to overlook the symbolic quality of all that belongs to the world of space and time, and lose sight of his true end and goal. As the passage shows, Pascal is at one with Plato in the primarily moral character of his concern that men should rise beyond the symbols to contemplate the higher reality they veil.[8] By allowing finite objects, harmless enough in themselves, to be mistaken for the end of life, man's attention is kept fixed on mere 'images', so that he has no eyes to see the true reality. This means that in Pascal's terms the physical universe cannot be regarded as interesting or valuable in its own right without undermining its symbolic purpose.

A notable example of the application of this Platonic theme to a concrete instance, which brings out the underlying valuation, occurs in another letter to Mme Périer, where Pascal discusses her husband's

---

[6] In the *Pensées* Pascal represents the "Sagesse du Dieu" as saying to man: "vous n'êtes plus maintenant en l'état où je vous ai formés. J'ai créé l'homme saint, innocent, parfait; je l'ai rempli de lumière et d'intelligence; je lui ai communiqué ma gloire et mes merveilles. L'œil de l'homme voyait alors la majesté de Dieu. Il n'était pas alors dans les ténèbres qui l'aveuglent, ..." L. 149; B. 430.

[7] C. pp. 484-5; G.E. II, p. 250.

[8] Cf. R. L. Nettleship, *The Theory of Education in the 'Republic' of Plato*, in *Hellenica*, ed. E. Abbott, London 1880, pp. 154-5.

building plans. He objects to the extravagance of these: if carried out they will require Périer to go for a considerable period of time without turning his mind to anything else, so that he will end by devoting to the building operation

... le temps qu'il faudrait pour se détromper des charmes secrets qui s'y trouvent.[9]

Pascal urges Mme Périer to take thought on the matter, and to encourage her husband to limit himself to the bare necessity

... de peur qu'il arrive qu'il ait bien plus de prudence et qu'il donne bien plus de soin et de peine au bâtiment d'une maison qu'il n'est pas obligé de faire, qu'à celui de cette tour mystique, donc tu sais que saint Augustin parle dans une de ses lettres, ...[10]

Man must always be on his guard, therefore, against getting ensnared in worldly concerns which will blind him to the reality behind and above them. The danger to which such an elaborate project exposes Périer is that he will become so caught up in this inessential and purely worldly enterprise that he will neglect, and eventually lose all sight of, what alone is essential and has reality.

A further passage from the previous letter also illustrates the way in which this Platonic view of the symbolism of the sensible world helps to qualify Pascal's appreciation of it. After the warning about the idolatry of setting up objects from the natural order as the supreme goal of desire, he continues

... ceux à qui Dieu fait connaître ces grandes vérités doivent user de ces images pour jouir de Celui qu'elles représentent, et ne demeurer pas éternellement dans cet aveuglement charnel et judaïque qui fait prendre la figure pour la réalité.[11]

Once again the injunction to penetrate to the reality shadowed forth by the images implies that the supernatural order is alone truly real, while the sensible world, by contrast, amounts to no more than 'figures'.[12] But perhaps more important here is Pascal's use of the two verbs "user" and "jouir" to distinguish the sort of attitude appropriate to the sensible and the supernatural. This shows that he is familiar with, and endorses, Saint Augustine's division of things into the two categories of use and enjoyment.[13] By this classification all goods short of the supreme good

[9] C. p. 489; G.E. II, p. 383.
[10] C. p. 490; G.E. II, p. 383.
[11] C. p. 485; G.E. II, p. 251.
[12] Cf. above, pp.7 ff.
[13] Cf. *De Doctrina Christiana,* I, iv, 4; I, xxii, 20; I, xxv, 39; II, xxiii, 36. Pascal seems to have been familiar with this treatise of Saint Augustine since he quotes from it in the *Pensées,* L. 251; B. 900.

are lumped together under the title of use. The reference to the "aveuglement charnel et judaïque" of those whose attention is rivetted to the
sensible image, so that it conceals instead of revealing the reality behind,
foreshadows the main theme of the doctrine of the "figuratifs" developed
in the *Pensées*. The error of the "Juifs charnels" is there seen to consist
precisely in their reversal of the true order of images and reality, use and
enjoyment.[14] In their 'cupidity' they enjoy what ought to be used, and
use what ought to be enjoyed, making reality subservient to images by
finding their end in what ought to be the means, and their means in
what ought to be the end.

... quand les biens sont promis en abondance, qui les empêchait d'entendre les
véritables biens, sinon leur cupidité, qui déterminait ce sens aux biens de la terre?
Mais ceux qui n'avaient de bien qu'en Dieu les rapportaient uniquement à Dieu.
Car il y a deux principes qui partagent les volontés des hommes, la cupidité et la
charité. Ce n'est pas que la cupidité ne puisse être avec la foi en Dieu et que la
charité ne soit avec les biens de la terre; mais la cupidité use de Dieu et jouit du
monde; et la charité, au contraire.[15]

By assigning whatever belongs to the world of here and now to the
category of use, so that it becomes a mere means to the attainment of an
end which lies outside its own order, Pascal again effectively deprives it
of all worth in itself.

Despite his insistence that the physical universe has value only as a
symbol, pointing to the existence of a spiritual reality behind and above
itself,[16] Pascal does not believe that men can discern this symbolic
quality simply by the exercise of their natural faculties. In the parable
of the prison the various 'images' and 'instructions', provided for the
captive to make good his escape, cannot be read correctly by the naked
human eye.

[14] Cf. above, p. 5.
[15] L. 502; B. 571. Cf. Saint Augustine, *De Doctrina Christiana*, III, x, 16: "I call
'charity' the motion of the soul toward the enjoyment of God for His own sake,
and the enjoyment of one's self and of one's neighbour for the sake of God; but
'cupidity' is a motion of the soul toward the enjoyment of one's self, one's neighbour, or any corporeal thing for the sake of something other than God." *De
Diversis Quaestionibus*, 30: "... all human perversity, or vice, consists in wishing
to enjoy what we ought to use, and to use what we ought to enjoy."
[16] Further references to this sacramental aspect of the world of nature occur
in the letters to Mlle de Roannez: "[Dieu] veut que nous jugions de la grâce par
la nature, ... C. p. 509: G.E. VI, p. 85. "... [le] secret de la nature qui couvre
[Dieu], ..." C. *ibid.*; G.E. VI; p. 87. "[Dieu] est demeuré caché sous le voile de la
nature qui nous le couvre jusqu'à l'Incarnation; ..." C. p. 510; G.E. VI, p. 88.
"Le voile de la nature qui couvre Dieu ..." C. *ibid.*; G.E. VI, p. 89, and in the
Pensées: "La nature a des perfections, pour montrer qu'elle est l'image de Dieu,
et des défauts, pour montrer qu'elle n'en est que l'image." L. 934; B. 580. "... la
conduite de Dieu est cachée sous la nature, comme en tous ses autres ouvrages."
L. 726; B. 876.

...mais il faut avouer qu'on ne peut apercevoir ces saints caractères sans une lumière surnaturelle; car comme toutes choses parlent de Dieu à ceux qui le connaissent, et qu'elles le découvrent à tous ceux qui l'aiment, ces mêmes choses le cachent à tous ceux qui ne le connaissent pas.[17]

The value of the physical world as a medium of revelation is therefore entirely relative; it will show a different face according as the observer who presents himself before it brings an eye already lightened by supernatural faith or not.[18] If he is a believer, the universe will appear to him as simply the means for expressing God's eternal reality; if not, it will be turned from a medium of instruction to an instrument of delusion, which ensnares him by captivating his senses, so that he becomes unable to see beyond to the true ground which lies behind.

Thus in the fourth letter to Mlle de Roannez, where Pascal insists at some length on the importance of the sacramental aspect of the sensible world, it is the Christians alone whom he considers capable of recognizing its symbolic reference.

Toutes choses couvrent quelque mystère; toutes choses sont des voiles qui couvrent Dieu. Les Chrétiens doivent le reconnaître en tout.[19]

---

[17] C. p. 484; G.E. II, p. 250.

[18] Saint Augustine likewise holds that the possibility of nature revealing its spiritual ground depends on the eye of the beholder. "All things are present to the blind as to the seeing. A blind man and one who hath sight, standing on the same spot, are each surrounded by the same form of things; but one is present to them, the other absent, ... not because the things themselves approach the one and recede from the other, but on account of the difference of their eyes. ... Thus also is God everywhere present, everywhere whole..." *Enarrationes in Psalmos*, XCIX, 5-6. "If a man merely stares at the world, while another not only sees but questions it, the world does not appear differently to them; but appearing the same to both, it is dumb to one and answers the other. Or rather it speaks to all, but only those can understand it who compare its answer with the truth that is within them." *Confessiones*, X, vi, 10.

[19] C. p. 510; G.E. VI, p. 89. The same point is made in a slightly different way in the *Pensées:* "Le monde subsiste pour exercer miséricorde et jugement, non pas comme si les hommes y étaient sortant des mains de Dieu, mais comme des ennemis de Dieu, auxquels il donne, par grâce, assez de lumière pour revenir, s'ils le veulent chercher et le suivre, mais pour les punir, s'ils refusent de le chercher..." L. 461; B. 584. Those whose eye has been enlightened by divine grace are therefore able to see in mere visible phenomena pointers beyond the world of sense to the spiritual reality: a condition which contrasts both with that of original righteousness, when no special gift of grace was necessary for man to perceive in the seen world an index to the unseen, and with that of the indifferent, for whom the material order constitutes simply a barrier to the spiritual since they have no inclination to seek after God. Thus in the first case the 'world', man's temporal surroundings, exercises a ministry of compassion by providing a pointer to the supernatural, while in the latter it acts as judgement, because men fail to take advantage of the opportunity it affords them of seeking for God. Cf. also L. 317; B. 701. L. 500; B. 700.

Only the Christian is able to see through and over the sensible appearances in this way to the reality which they veil. The world of nature lies open to his eye because it has been illuminated by divine grace, and is able to trace there the marks of the supernatural creator.

This ambivalent attitude toward the world of sensible phenomena, which derives from the notion of disparate orders of being, leaves no room for traditional natural theology.[20] Pascal will have no truck with arguments based on the conviction that nature can suggest to man the existence of God, or of a spiritual order, as an idea previously unknown to him.[21] In his terms spiritual things are spiritually discerned, so that members of the two lower orders of being are precluded from knowledge of them because they are blind to the values of the supernatural order which lie beyond their range of vision. It is inconceivable, then, that the "charnels" or the "savants" should be able by mere scrutiny to perceive the sacramental character of the world of nature; that world as seen by the spiritual man must necessarily be a very different world from the one seen by the carnal or intellectual man.

The spiritual illumination which accompanies faith produced by divine grace, opening man's eyes to what he could not otherwise see, is described in language that recalls the higher intellectual education outlined in *The Republic*. In Plato's scheme the eye of the soul is converted from the idols of the cave to the upper world of sunlight, and finally to

---

[20] Pascal breaks with the Augustinian tradition at this point. In Saint Augustine's scheme of creation, based on the Platonic doctrine of participation, there are degrees of reality, and all things are graded according to their likeness to God. Thus in *The City of God* he affirms that "... nothing in nature being evil, ... but everything from earth to heaven ascending in a scale of goodness, and so from the visible unto the invisible, unto which all are unequal. And in the greatest is God the great workman, yet no less is he in the less: which little things are not to be measured by their own greatness, being near to nothing, but by their Maker's wisdom: ..." XI, 12. Again in the same work he speaks of "running through all things under us (which could not be created, formed, nor ordered without the hand of the most essential, wise, and good God), and so through all the works of the creation; gathering from one more plain, and from another less apparent marks of his essence; ..." XI, 28. Moreover, unlike Pascal, Saint Augustine does not hesitate to appeal to the way in which natural objects reflect in their order, unity and beauty the unity and immutable perfection of God as proof of his existence: "For whithersoever thou turnest He speaks to thee by the marks which he has impressed on his works, and when thou art slipping back to exterior things, he recalls thee by the very forms of these things ... Gaze at the sky, the earth, the sea, and all the things which shine in them or above them, or creep or fly or swim beneath them. They have forms because they have rhythm; take this away and they will no longer be. From whom then are they save from him, from whom rhythm is; since they have being only in so far as they are rhythmically ordered." *De Libero Arbitrio* II, xvi. Cf. also *Confessiones*, XI, iv.

[21] Cf. *Pensées*, L. 3; B. 244. L. 449; B. 556. L. 781; B. 242.

the vision of the Good.[22] And Pascal's short treatise *Sur la conversion du pécheur* opens with the following statement:

La première chose que Dieu inspire à l'âme qu'il daigne toucher véritablement, est une connaissance et une vue tout extraordinaire par laquelle l'âme considère les choses et elle-même d'une façon toute nouvelle.[23]

After receiving this illumination, which transforms itself and its environment together, the soul undergoes an elevating process in the course of which it is converted from preoccupation with the goods of this world, and is finally brought to appreciate the values of the supernatural order.

... sa raison aidée de la lumière de la grâce lui fait connaître qu'il n'y a rien de plus aimable que Dieu...[24]

Pascal adopts here the traditional view of grace having a "tonic effect" on man's natural capacity as it "throws open a new world" consequent on the act of faith,[25] so that the Christian's eye is illuminated and then turned back on the world with transfigured sight.

This function of grace as a sort of tonic acting on man's natural faculties, revealing fresh perspectives to the eye of the believer, is further emphasized in a rather different context in a letter to Mme Périer. Pascal is discussing the ability to perceive the spiritual significance, not of the world of sensible phenomena, but of texts from Scripture.

... pour y entendre ce langage secret et étranger à ceux qui le sont du ciel, il faut que la même grâce, qui peut seule en donner la première intelligence, la continue et la rende toujours présente... car notre mémoire, aussi bien que les instructions qu'elle retient, n'est qu'un corps inanimé et judaïque sans l'esprit qui les doit vivifier.[26]

By insisting in this way on the need for the spiritualized insight of faith for man to be able to trace the marks of the supernatural in the world of nature, Pascal is in effect doing little more than reaffirm the disparateness of the different orders of being. The notion that man is capable of reaching to a knowledge of God, or of the supernatural order, through his own efforts runs counter to the whole gist of that conception. This explains Pascal's insistence that awareness of the supernatural can only

---

[22] *The Republic*, VII, 514A-521B. Cf. R. L. Nettleship, *The Theory of Education in the 'Republic' of Plato*, pp. 157ff. Nettleship actually remarks that "The general principle, then, of the higher education is expressed in the term 'conversion'." p. 157.

[23] C. p. 548; G.E. X, p. 422.

[24] C. p. 550; G.E. X, p. 425.

[25] Cf. Dom Illtyd Trethowan, *An Essay in Christian Philosophy*, London 1954, pp. 14-17.

[26] C. pp. 488-9; G.E. II, pp. 379-381.

come about in the first instance as the result of a discovery by God of himself to man.[27]

Despite the fact, therefore, that Pascal arranges his orders of being in a hierarchy according to their appropriate values, and that he believes the meanest material forms belonging to the corporeal order represent the supernatural reality, because they partake in some measure in the unity which is truly realized only in God,[28] the gulf remains unbridged between the different points of view from which he makes his often seemingly inconsistent judgements. Since he stipulates that it is only to the true spiritual eye, illuminated by grace, that natural phenomena reveal their relation to the supernatural, the symbolism of the natural order simply adds a further dimension to the relativity of his scale. The mere fact that to the Christian's eye the visible is in every part a revelation of the invisible, so that he sees even in the things of the natural order a witness to the supernatural, does not break down the duality. Looked at by itself the natural order still shows varying degrees of positive worth; but when considered in relation to the supernatural order all is changed, and it appears as in itself worthless. Thus, just as in Pascal's scheme of reality there is no step by step rise from a lower order to a higher one through a 'chain of being', so also at the critical points in his scale of values differences of degree become negligible in the face of radical differences of kind.

---

[27] Cf. *Pensées:* "La foi est un don de Dieu. Ne croyez pas que nous disions que c'est un don de raisonnement." L. 588; B. 279. ". . . il est impossible que Dieu soit jamais la fin, s'il n'est le principe." L. 988; B. 488. *De l'esprit géométrique:* "Dieu seul peut mettre [les vérités divines] dans l'âme, et par la manière qu'il lui plaît." C. p. 592; G.E. IX, pp. 271-2.

[28] C. p. 485; G.E. II, p. 250. Cf. above, p. 87.

BIBLIOGRAPHY

Abercrombie, N. J. *The Origins of Jansenism,* Oxford, 1936.
—. *Saint Augustine and French Classical Thought,* Oxford, 1938.
Adam, A. *Histoire de la littérature française au XVIIe siècle,* 5 vols., Paris, 1948-56.
—. *Sur le problème religieux dans la première moitié du XVIIe siècle,* Oxford, 1959.
Angers, J. E. d' *Pascal et ses précurseurs,* Paris, 1954.
Arnauld, A. *Œuvres,* 43 vols., Paris and Lausanne, 1775-83.
Bénichou, P. *Morales du grand siècle,* Paris, 1948.
Blondel, M. *Le jansénisme et l'anti-jansénisme de Pascal, Revue de métaphysique et de morale,* 1923, pp. 129-163.
Boase, A. M. *The Fortunes of Montaigne,* London, 1935.
Bremond, H. *Histoire littéraire du sentiment religieux en France,* 11 vols., Paris, 1916-33.
—. *Autour de l'humanisme. D'Erasme à Pascal,* Paris, 1936.
Broome, J. H. *Pascal,* London, 1965.
Brunschvicg, L. *Descartes et Pascal lecteurs de Montaigne,* New York, 1944.
—. *Blaise Pascal,* Paris, 1953.
Burnaby, J. *Amor Dei: A Study of the Religion of Saint Augustine,* London, 1938.
Busson, H. *La pensée religieuse française de Charron à Pascal,* Paris, 1933.
—. *La religion des classiques (1660-1685),* Paris, 1948.
Cahiers de Royaumont. Blaise Pascal, l'homme et l'œuvre, Paris, 1956.
Cassirer, E. *The Philosophy of the Enlightenment,* Boston, 1955.
Chevalier, J. *Pascal,* Paris, 1922.
Chinard, G. *En lisant Pascal,* Lille and Geneva, 1948.
Cognet, L. *La réforme de Port-Royal (1591-1618),* Paris, 1950.
—. *La Mère Angélique et Saint François de Sales (1618-1626),* Paris, 1951.
Collingwood, R. G. *An Essay on Philosophical Method,* Oxford, 1933.
Courcelle, P. *L'entretien de Pascal et Sacy. Ses sources et ses énigmes,* Paris, 1960.

Dagens, J. *Bérulle et les origines de la restauration catholique* (1575-1611), Paris, 1952.

Delassault, G. *Le Maistre de Sacy et son temps,* Paris, 1957.

Demorest, J. J. *L'honnête homme et le croyant selon Pascal, Modern Philology,* vol. 53, no. 4, 1956, pp. 217-20.

Descartes, R. *Œuvres et lettres,* ed. A. Bridoux, Paris, 1953.

Domat, J. *Les loix civiles dans leur ordre naturel,* new ed., Paris, 1735.

Droz, E. *Etude sur le scepticisme de Pascal,* Paris, 1886.

Fletcher, F. T. H. *Pascal and the Mystical Tradition,* Oxford, 1954.

Gaiffe, F. *L'envers du grand siècle,* Paris, 1924.

Gazier, A. *Blaise Pascal et Antoine Escobar: Etude historique et critique,* Paris, 1912.

Gilson, E. *Introduction à l'étude de Saint Augustin,* 2nd ed., Paris, 1943.

—. *L'esprit de la philosophie médiévale,* 2nd ed., Paris, 1944.

Goldmann, L. *Le Dieu caché,* Paris, 1955.

Gouhier, H. *La pensée religieuse de Descartes,* Paris, 1924.

—. *Essais sur Descartes,* 2nd ed., Paris, 1949.

—. *Blaise Pascal commentaires,* Paris, 1966.

Gounelle, A. *L'entretien de Pascal avec Monsieur de Sacy, étude et commentaire,* Paris, 1966.

James, E. D. *Pierre Nicole, Jansenist and Humanist,* The Hague, 1972.

Jansenius, C. *Augustinus,* Louvain, 1640, Frankfurt/Main, 1964.

Jovy, E. *Etudes pascaliennes,* 9 vols., Paris, 1927-36.

Kirk, K. E. *The Vision of God: The Christian Doctrine of the Summum Bonum,* London, 1931.

Krailsheimer, A. J. *Studies in Self-Interest from Descartes to La Bruyère,* Oxford, 1962.

Lanson, G. *La transformation des idées morales et la naissance des morales rationnelles de 1680 à 1715, Revue du mois,* 1910, pp. 5-28.

Laporte, J. *Pascal et la doctrine de Port-Royal, Revue de Métaphysique et de morale,* 1923, pp. 247-306.

—. *Le cœur et la raison selon Pascal,* Paris, 1950.

—. *La doctrine de Port Royal,* 4 vols., Paris, 1923-52.

Levi, A. H. T. *French Moralists. The theory of the passions 1585 to 1649,* Oxford, 1964.

Lovejoy, A. O. *The Great Chain of Being,* Cambridge Mass., 1936.

—. *Reflections on Human Nature,* Baltimore, 1961.

McAdoo, H. R. *The Structure of Caroline Moral Theology,* London, 1949.

Magendie, M. *La politesse mondaine et les théories de l'honnêteté, en France, au XVIIe siècle, de 1600 à 1660,* 2 vols., Paris, 1925.

Méré, A. G. Chevalier de, *Œuvres complètes,* ed. C-H. Boudhors, 3 vols., Paris, 1930.

Mesnard, J. *Pascal, l'homme et l'œuvre,* Paris, 1951.

—. *Pascal et les Roannez,* 2 vols., Paris, 1965.

—. *Pascal et le problème moral, L'information littéraire,* 1966, pp. 1-7.

Mesnard, P. *Essai sur la morale de Descartes,* Paris, 1936.

Miel, J. *Pascal and Theology,* Baltimore and London, 1969.

Montaigne, M. de, *Essais,* ed. P. Villey, Paris, 1965.

Morel, J. *Réflexions sur le sentiment pascalien, Revue des sciences humaines,* 1960, pp. 21-29.

Nicole, P. *Essais de morale,* 14 vols., Paris, 1682-1755.

Orcibal, J. *Les origines du Jansénisme,* 5 vols., Paris, 1947-62.

Pascal, B. *Œuvres complètes,* ed. L. Brunschvicg, P. Boutroux, and F. Gazier, 14 vols., Paris, 1908-25.

—. *Pensées et opuscules,* ed. L. Brunschvicg, 7th ed., Paris 1914.

—. *Œuvres complètes,* ed. J. Chevalier, Paris, 1957.

—. *Les Provinciales,* ed. L. Cognet, Paris, 1965.

—. *Œuvres complètes,* ed. J. Mesnard, vols. I and II, Paris, 1964-70.

Pascal présent 1662-1962, Clermont-Ferrand, 1962.

Pellisson, M. *La sécularisation de la morale au XVIIIe siècle, La révolution française,* 1903, pp. 385-408.

Pintard, R. *Le libertinage érudit dans la première moitié du XVIIe siècle,* 2 vols., Paris, 1943.

Portalié, E. *Saint Augustin,* in *Dictionnaire de Théologie Catholique,* vol. I, Paris, 1902.

Potts, D. C. *Pascal's contemporaries and "le divertissement", Modern Language Review,* 1962, pp. 31-40.

Prigent, J. *La conception pascalienne de l'ordre,* in *Ordre, désordre, lumière,* (Collège philosophique), Paris, 1952.

Rashdall, H. *The Theory of Good and Evil,* 2 vols., 2nd ed., Oxford, 1924.

Rauh, F. *La Philosophie de Pascal, Revue de métaphysique et de morale,* 1923, pp. 307-344.

Raymond, M. *Du Jansénisme à la morale de l'intérêt, Mercure de France,* June, 1957, pp. 238-255.

Rodis-Lewis, G. *La morale de Descartes,* Paris, 1957.

Rohmer, J. *La finalité morale chez les théologiens de Saint Augustin à Duns Scot,* Paris, 1939.

Roland-Gosselin, B. *La morale de Saint Augustin,* Paris, 1925.

Rolland, E. *La loi de réalisation humaine dans Saint Thomas,* Paris, 1935.

Russier, J. *La foi selon Pascal,* 2 vols., Paris, 1949.

—. *Sagesse cartésienne et religion,* Paris, 1958.

Sainte-Beuve, C. A. *Port-Royal,* ed. M. Leroy, 3 vols., Paris, 1952-5.

Sellier, P. *Pascal et Saint Augustin,* Paris, 1970.

Sertillanges, A-D. *La philosophie morale de Saint Thomas D'Aquin,* Paris, 1916.

Smith, N. K. *New Studies in the Philosophy of Descartes,* London, 1952.

Souilhé, J. *Les idées de Pascal sur la morale, Archives de philosophie,* vol. I, cahier 3, 1923, pp. 68-91.

Spink, J. S. *French Free-Thought from Gassendi to Voltaire,* London, 1960.

Stace, W. T. *Time and Eternity. An Essay in the Philosophy of Religion*, Princeton, 1952.

Stewart, H. F. *Les Provinciales de Blaise Pascal*, Manchester, 1920.

Thomas, J-F. *Essai sur la morale de Port-Royal*, Paris, 1942.

—. *Le problème moral à Port-Royal*, Paris, 1963.

Tourneur, Z. *Une vie avec Blaise Pascal*, Paris, 1943.

Trethowan, I. *An Essay in Christian Philosophy*, London, 1954.

Verneaux, R. *La doctrine pascalienne des trois ordres, Revue de philosophie*, 1938, pp. 310-43.

Vinet, A. *Etudes sur Blaise Pascal*, 5th ed., Lausanne, 1936.

Webb, C. C. J. *Kant's Philosophy of Religion*, Oxford, 1926.

—. *Pascal's Philosophy of Religion*, Oxford, 1929.

Wicksteed, P. H. *The Reactions between Dogma and Philosophy Illustrated from the Works of S. Thomas Aquinas*, London, 1920.

Williams, N. P. *The Ideas of the Fall and of Original Sin*, London, 1927.

—. *The Grace of God*, London, 1930.

Wood, T. *English Casuistical Divinity during the Seventeenth Century*, London, 1952.

INDEX

INDEX